W9-BUG-242

Sponge Painting

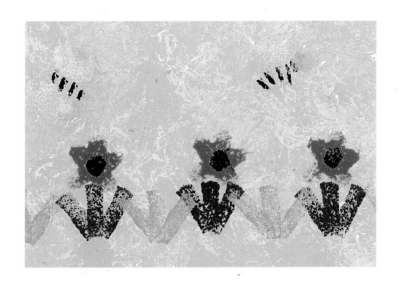

Emily Williston Memorial Library
DISCARDED
Easthampton, MA

Sponge Painting

ANN ROONEY

DISCARDED

THE GUILD OF MASTER CRAFTSMAN PUBLICATIONS LTD

First published 1999 by
Guild of Master Craftsman Publications Ltd,
166 High Street, Lewes,
East Sussex BN7 1XU

© GMC Publications Ltd 1999
Text and illustrations © Ann Rooney 1999

ISBN 1 86108 134 0

All rights reserved

The right of Ann Rooney to be identified as the author
of this work has been asserted in accordance with the
Copyright Designs and Patents Act 1988, Sections 77 and 78.

No part of this publication may be reproduced, stored in a
retrieval system, or transmitted in any form or by any means
without the prior permission of the publisher and copyright owner.

This book is sold subject to the condition that all designs are
copyright and are not for commercial reproduction without
permission of the designer and copyright owner.

The publishers and author can accept no legal responsibility
for any consequences arising from the application of
information, advice or instructions given in this publication.

A catalogue record of this book is available from the British Library.

Photographer: Christine Richardson
Designer (cover): Ian Smith, Guild of Master Craftsman Publications Design Studio
Designer: Sarah Theodosiou
Editor: Andy Charman
Line illustrator: Robert Layzell
Typefaces: Palatino and Meta
Colour origination by Viscan Graphics (Singapore)
Printed and bound by Kyodo Printing (Singapore)
under the supervision of MRM Graphics, Winslow, Buckinghamshire, UK

Contents

Introduction

If you feel that you would like to embark on a new hobby, are keen to use paints, but do not have the time to learn complicated painting techniques, then sponge painting will be the ideal medium for you.

No brush skills are required. Sponge painting is a simple method of printing a design using blocks cut from household foam sponges. This medium produces highly individual textural effects quite unlike those produced by other printing methods. The most important factor involved in this technique is an effective use of colour to create dramatic contracts and subtle textures.

The possibilities for free expression and experimentation are unlimited and I hope that when using this book you will find the necessary encouragement to develop many exciting designs of your own.

No costly equipment is needed and all the materials required are easily obtainable. If you are seeking projects to decorate, you may choose an environmentally friendly approach by selecting second-hand items. Unusual and interesting pieces can often be found at boot fairs and jumble sales. You will soon become expert at recognizing the potential of an object which might at first glance appear to be unpromising. A second-hand item can be swiftly transformed into something special. All that is needed is a little acrylic paint and a few foam sponges.

If you are seeking new items to decorate, then a wide variety of products are readily available. Hobby magazines, for example, carry advertisements for suppliers of wooden and metal blanks. I am sure that you will find many items, which are both practical and decorative. The flexibility of the sponge painting technique means that you can adapt the designs featured in this book to decorate the project of your choice.

I hope that you will enjoy using this book and will be able to spend many creative hours with paints and sponges.

CHAPTER 1

Materials and Equipment

Sponge painting requires no expensive equipment and all the materials used are readily available at DIY stores and from art and crafts suppliers. Many of the items listed here you will probably already own, tucked away in toolboxes and kitchen cupboards.

The basic equipment described here will be needed to complete all the projects in the book. Specific paint colours and additional requirements will be listed in each project chapter.

BASIC EQUIPMENT

• **Scissors**

You will need a small, sharp-pointed pair

of scissors for cutting out the printing blocks. In addition, a larger pair of household scissors will be necessary for cutting out the cardboard templates and any other rough work.

- **Tracing paper**
- **Cardboard**
- **A soft pencil e.g. 2B**
- **Felt-tipped pen**

These items will be needed for preparing the templates.

- **Household paintbrushes**

These are for painting your projects and for priming and finishing.

- **Watercolour brushes**

These brushes will be used for painting the colour on to the sponge printing blocks. Inexpensive brushes, such as those designed for a child's use, will be adequate for this purpose. You will find it useful to have a selection of these brushes in different sizes.

- **Masking tape**
- **Scrap paper**

These items will be useful for designing the positioning and spacing of motifs on a project.

- **Old newspapers**

You will need plenty of old newspapers to protect your work surface and for testing printing.

- **Roll of absorbent kitchen paper**

A roll of kitchen paper will be invaluable for wiping brushes, mopping up spills, etc. Kitchen paper will also be an important requirement for some of the decorative paint effects.

- **Paint-mixing dishes**

Old saucers or foil pie dishes make ideal mixing palettes.

- **Plastic picnic spoons**

A plastic picnic spoon is ideal for scooping small quantities of emulsion paint from the tin.

- **Clingfilm**

It is a good idea to cover dishes of mixed paint with clingfilm to prevent the paint from drying out.

- **Jam jar**

You will need a jar to hold water for washing brushes.

- **Foam scouring sponges**

Small sponge scouring pads are readily available at supermarkets and other shops. Look for a pad with a close textured sponge and a good stiff scouring layer on the base. This strong base makes the sponge-printing block easy to handle and enables you to exert an even pressure when printing. The sponge pads usually measure 8 x 6cm (3⅛ x 2⅜in) and have depth of 4cm (1⁹⁄₁₆in).

Additional Materials

All additional materials required to complete individual projects will be listed in the appropriate project chapter.

long service. After use, wash your sponge in warm water and allow it to dry naturally.

- **Ruler or tape measure**

These are useful for calculating the spacing between a repeated design.

- **Wax polish**
- **Sandpaper**

These items will be needed when creating a distressed paint finish.

Paint

A variety of different types of water-based paints have been used to decorate the projects in this book. The different types of paint can be mixed together quite happily.

- **Emulsion paint**

Standard emulsion paint with a matt finish is suitable for base-coating projects and can also be used for printing the designs. It is well worth asking friends and relatives to donate all their left over scraps of emulsion paint. To save space, I store such small quantities of emulsion paint in old screw-topped jars.

The 50ml (1.69fl.oz) sample pots of emulsion paint are a good buy and are available in a wide range of colours in most DIY stores.

It is not necessary to rush out and buy lots of different colours at first, because many colours can be mixed from a few basic sample pots. This will save you something on your expenses.

- **Sheet foam**

High-density sheet foam can be used to make large printing blocks. It can be obtained from upholstery shops and suppliers. Odd-shaped off-cuts are often free of charge or a nominal fee.

- **Plastic bags**
- **Bubble wrap**

You will need these items when creating some of the decorative paint effects.

- **Natural sea sponge**

These sponges can be quite expensive to buy, but if treated carefully, will give

To begin with, it is worth investing in the following: a small tin of red (scarlet or similar), dark blue (ultramarine or similar), and a bright yellow (cadmium yellow or similar). In addition, you will need white and a small pot of black. DIY stores which have a paint-mixing facility will mix a minimum quantity of one litre (33.8fl.oz) of emulsion paint.

Acrylic paints for decorative painting are available in a large range of very beautiful colours. You may prefer to buy some of these small 59ml (2fl.oz) pots of acrylic paint to begin with.

Some of the projects in this book have been decorated with metallic acrylic paints. In addition to the usual gold,

silver and bronze, these paints are available in many lovely colours, all with a pearly metallic finish. These types of acrylic paint are available from good art and crafts shops and mail order suppliers. In addition, because of the renewed interest in DIY and craft, many of the larger DIY stores now also carry this type of paint as well as many other essential pieces of equipment and optional extras.

- **Priming paints**
- **Varnish**

The use of these materials for priming and finishing projects is discussed fully in Chapters 2 and 3.

CHAPTER 2

Preparing Surfaces

I use objects made of different materials in my work and these need to be prepared and primed in different ways before painting can begin.

WOOD

Second-hand items may need to be stripped of old paint or varnish. Use a proprietary brand of paint stripper for this and follow the manufacturer's instructions carefully.

Smooth any rough edges with sandpaper and prime with a wood priming paint.

New items made from wood or medium-density fibreboard (MDF) can be primed as for second-hand items or can be given two coats of white emulsion paint as a base.

METAL

Old metal will usually need to be treated against rust. Use a wire brush to remove all traces of rust and loose, flaky material. Coat with a rust-inhibiting primer.

New metal will require only a coat of metal-priming paint.

CLAY FLOWERPOTS

Clay pots need to be sealed before painting, to prevent the paint from being absorbed into the porous material. I use acrylic varnish for this. Mix the varnish with a little water and brush on to the pot. Two coats of sealant will usually be sufficient to provide a good base for painting.

FABRIC

Natural fabrics such as cotton, silk and linen are the first choice for fabric painting. Artificial fibres do not take the paint well.

Before use, always wash the fabric to remove any dressing, then dry and iron in the usual way.

Many types of fabric paint are available at art and craft shops and from mail order suppliers. Always follow the manufacturer's instructions, because these products vary considerably in their make-up and application.

In addition, a textile medium can be mixed with some brands of acrylic paint to produce fabric paint.

PAPER AND CARD

Sponge painting can be used to decorate all types of paper products. Greetings cards, box files, cardboard containers, notebooks, photo albums and papier-mâché are all suitable. Paper products need no special preparation before painting.

CHAPTER 3

Finishing

The choice of materials for finishing your projects is largely a matter of personal taste. For some projects however, their purpose will dictate the type of finishing product used.

POLYURETHANE VARNISH

This material gives a very durable finish and is suitable for sealing and protecting projects that are likely to receive a lot of wear and tear. Furniture such as the child's table and the tea tray project would benefit from being finished with several coats of polyurethane varnish. Apply the varnish with a paintbrush and allow it to dry thoroughly between coats. Follow the manufacturer's instructions carefully as this type of varnish is flammable and needs to be used only in a well-ventilated space. After use, brushes need to be cleaned with white spirit.

ACRYLIC VARNISH

This water-based varnish is very quick drying, has very little odour and is easier to use than polyurethane varnish.

An added advantage is that brushes can be cleaned with water.

Acrylic varnish is suitable for finishing all projects that will be subject to medium wear and tear.

Both these types of varnish are available in gloss, silk or matt finishes. I usually use a matt finish for completing my work but this is just a matter of personal preference.

WAX POLISH

Decorative paintwork can also be sealed with a beeswax furniture polish or brushing wax. Apply the wax to the painted surface with a soft cloth and leave for 30 minutes to allow the wax to penetrate into the paint. Apply a second coat of wax and finish by buffing with a soft cloth.

Antique wax, which is brown in appearance, can also be used to give projects a traditional, aged look. This is particularly suitable for use over the top of a distressed paint finish to give an authentic rustic farmhouse 'feel' to your piece of work.

CHAPTER 4

Using and Adapting the Designs

This book will show you how to produce all the designs shown. What you decorate, however, is up to you. For example, you may choose to paint a large flowerpot with the grapevine design or to cover a table top with sunflowers.

Your choice may well depend on available objects and an existing colour scheme. If you have an old metal waste bin crying out for refurbishment and one of the designs given for flowerpots exactly matches your bedroom décor, then you can easily adapt the flowerpot design to decorate the bin.

If you like the peaches design, but would prefer a minimalist look, why not paint a single motif of one peach backed by a small group of leaves? This small motif could be used successfully to decorate any project.

Designs can be adapted to decorate objects of many different shapes and sizes. Don't be afraid to enlarge or reduce the designs by cutting the printing blocks larger or smaller than the templates given in the book. With a little practise, you will soon master this.

At the conclusion of each project chapter, I have included ideas for

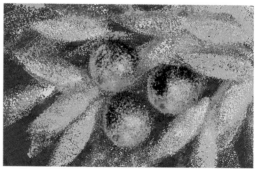

With an application of light orange paint and green to represent the reflection of the leaves, the peaches in Chapter 18 become oranges; by using red and a touch of green, they become apples.

changing and adapting each design. Guidelines will be given for alternative colour schemes and for alterations to the given designs. Often, surprisingly different results can be obtained by making quite small changes and additions.

I hope that this will widen the scope of the book and encourage an adventurous approach to sponge painting.

When altering and adapting designs there are a few guidelines that may be useful to bear in mind:
• Try not to overcrowd the design. Often the spaces between the images are an important aspect of the overall appearance of the design.
• When grouping images together – sunflower blooms for example – an odd number of flowers will group together more harmoniously than an even number.

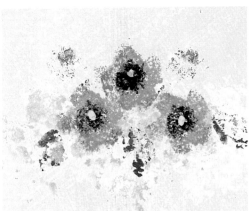
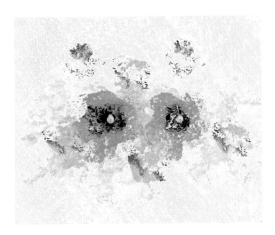
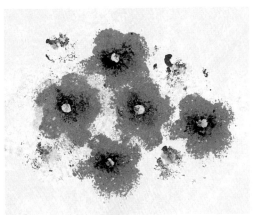

An even number of flower motifs do not group together well, whereas an odd number of flower motifs group together with much greater harmony.

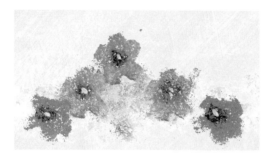

Unequal spacing gives this design a natural appearance.

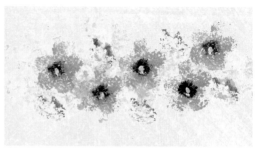

Untidy positioning makes this design appear unbalanced.

Adequate spacing creates a balanced design.

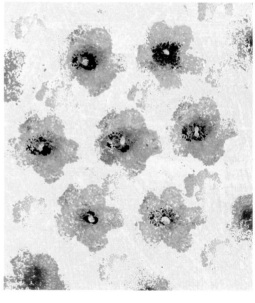

Here, the motifs are positioned too closely, giving the design an overcrowded appearance.

If you are using a geometric design, you will need to measure your project to ensure that the repeated design fits exactly. Measure the template and calculate the number of times that the repeated design will be accommodated. You can adjust the space between the motifs if necessary, or you can enlarge or reduce the size of the template.

If you are decorating a circular object, a flowerpot, for example, the easiest way to measure is with a piece of string or tape. Wrap the string in a straight line

around the circumference of the pot
where your design will be printed. Mark
the string at the point where the ends
meet. Make sure that the string is pulled
tightly around the pot and is straight or
your measurement will be inaccurate.
The length of the string represents the
length that your design will cover.
Measure the string and the template and
calculate the design requirements as
before. Use a soft pencil to mark the
positions for the design on your project.

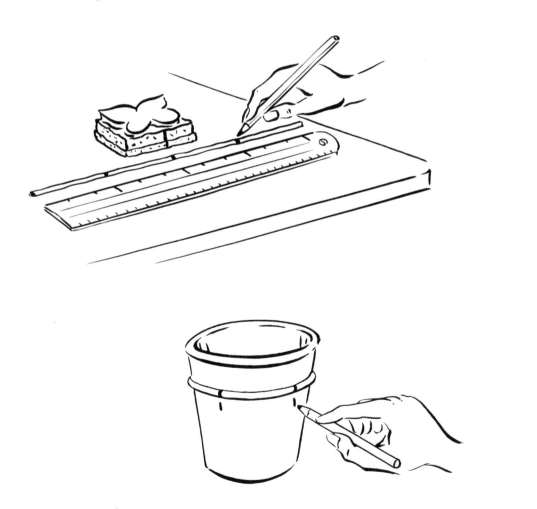

CHAPTER 5

Preparing the Printing Blocks

All the designs in this book are built up by using very simple shapes. Leaves, petals, fruit, and so on, are represented in a very basic manner. These simple shapes can easily be drawn free hand onto the sponge scouring pads. If you do not feel confident enough to attempt free hand drawing, then proceed as follows:

1 Use tracing paper and a soft pencil (2B is ideal) to trace the outline of the template required.

2 Turn the tracing paper over and lay it on to the surface of a piece of card. Re-trace the outline of the template shape, or scribble over the surface with a soft pencil, to transfer the template shape on to the card. (Old cereal packets will provide cardboard that is perfectly adequate for this purpose.)

3 Cut out the cardboard shape.

4 Place the cardboard shape on to the sponge surface of a scouring pad. Draw around the outline of the shape with a felt-tipped pen.

Don't worry if the shape you have cut appears a little ragged; sponge painting does not require sharp, precise images. Much of its appeal lies in a very free and spontaneous appearance, not in formal or rigid lines.

5 To cut out the printing block, you will need to use small, sharp-pointed scissors. Dig the lower point of the scissors into the sponge and carefully snip around your outlined shape.

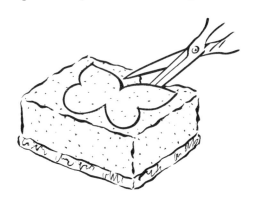

7 If you are attempting a larger design and sponge-scouring pads are too small for your needs, you can cut your design from sheet foam. When you have cut out your shapes you will need to glue them onto a cardboard base. This will give you a firm base to press down on when printing. (You will need to check that the glue used is suitable for sticking plastic foam.)

6 Gradually snip away the unwanted portion of the sponge, to leave your template shape standing proud of the base. Use a larger pair of scissors to cut through the tough layer at the base of the scouring pad.

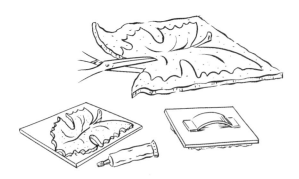

If you're cutting small template shapes, such as grapes, berries and flowers, cut away the sides of the sponge straight through to the base, leaving little or no margin around your shape. This makes it easier to align your shape accurately when printing.

If you're cutting thin strips of sponge to print flower stems, leaf fronds, grass stems, etc., you will not need to include the stiff base on such a tiny printing block. The sponge alone is quite adequate for printing very thin lines such as these.

CHAPTER 6

Printing

The templates provided for each project include a basic colour guide to applying the paint to the sponge printing blocks. Background colour, shading and highlights are all indicated in these guides.

Here's how to do the printing:

1 Begin by painting the background colour directly on to the sponge printing block, using a watercolour paintbrush. The absorbent sponge will soak up the paint; therefore apply several brush loads, taking care that the edges of the block are well covered. Then add any contrasting colours as indicated in the colour guide. Use a thin watercolour brush to apply fine lines and highlights.

2 Before printing onto your project piece always test stamp onto newspaper first. This will blot any excess paint. (You do not want the paint to appear too heavy or too blobby in texture.) It will also blend the colours together, giving a subtle mixture and softening the effect.

3 Press your printing block down gently onto the surface of your project, rocking the sponge slightly from side to side and from top to bottom. This will ensure that the edges of the motif are crisply printed. Take care not to slide the sponge from its original position, which will cause the image to become blurred.

Reload your sponge with paint following steps 1 and 2 when the printing becomes faint. Remember to test print onto newspaper after every fresh application of paint.

It is worth taking a little time to practise the printing process before commencing each project. This will help you to get the feel of the paint and to study the effects of the varying textures. Use scrap paper for this practice.

A very light pressure on a relatively dry sponge will give the impression of distance to the work (see the background trees in the forest design on page 19).

Use the opposite technique – heavier pressure and a full load of paint – when printing foreground detail.

If you make a mistake, wipe off the paint with a wad of damp kitchen paper, dry and print again. You will have to be quick though, because acrylic paint dries rapidly. If you are unhappy with a section of your work after the paint has dried, repaint the offending area with the background colour. Apply any paint effects and reprint the section of the design.

Printing blocks cut from scouring pads can be used many times. When you have finished printing, wash out the sponges in warm water and squeeze them dry.

Large printing blocks cut from sheet foam and glued to a cardboard base can be used once only.

Applying light pressure to a sponge which is quite dry gives an impression of distance to the background leaves. Heavier pressure and a full load of paint brings the foreground leaves 'forward'.

CHAPTER 7

Decorative Paint Effects

Before applying any of the decorative paint effects that follow, you will need to apply a base coat to your project with emulsion or acrylic paint. This will provide a good background for the effects. Apply two or more coats, allowing the paint to dry between coats.

SPONGING ON

The sponging on method works well when the colour used for sponging is a few tones lighter or darker than the background colour. A contrasting colour, or colours, can also be used and will give dramatic results.

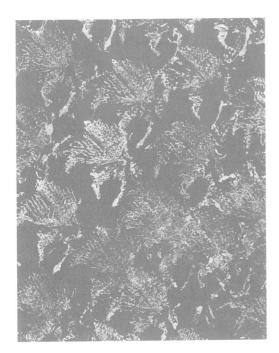

Sponging on with kitchen paper – light on dark.

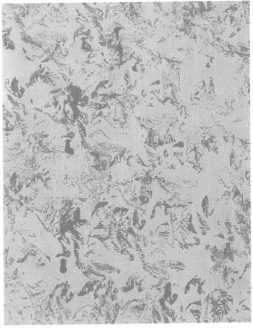

Sponging on with kitchen paper – dark on light.

Begin by mixing your paint in a flat dish or saucer. Take two or three sheets of kitchen paper and crumple them into a crinkly ball.

Dip the ball of paper into the paint and gently press the painted part onto your project. Repeat this dabbing motion to apply the paint in splodges, evenly spaced, to completely cover the base coat.

Re-fold the paper if it becomes worn and saturated with paint, or crumple a new ball of paper if necessary.

When your surface is covered and you are satisfied with the result of your sponging, set the project aside to dry.

If you choose to use a piece of natural sea sponge instead of paper, you will need to dampen the sponge before use and squeeze out any excess water. Dip the sponge into the paint and proceed in exactly the same way as described for the paper method.

I prefer natural sponge because it gives a more delicate and intricate pattern than the paper method.

SPONGING OFF
This method works particularly well when a metallic paint is sponged over a matt finish base coat. It will produce a very contemporary effect.

Sponging on with a piece of natural sea sponge.

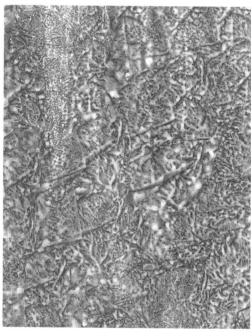

Sponging off with kitchen paper.

Begin by diluting the metallic paint with a little water. (Mix only a small amount at a time to avoid wastage.) Using a soft brush, paint this water mixture over the base coat.

Crumple some kitchen paper into a ball and dab this over the painted surface. The paper will remove some of the paint, exposing the contrasting base colour, and form a crinkly pattern on the surface. Repeat the dabbing process until you are happy with the pattern you have achieved.

THE PLASTIC BAG METHOD
Brush over the base coat with a diluted mixture of contrasting paint just as described for the sponging off method above. Crumple a plastic bag, inside out, so that no print comes off into the paint, and use this to sponge off the paint onto your project. The plastic will not remove as much of the top layer of paint as the paper method did, but will leave a rippled pattern on the surface. You can experiment freely with the ball of plastic to make all kinds of interesting patterns such as wavy lines, swirls and so on.

THE BUBBLE WRAP METHOD
Dab over the painted surface with a pad of folded bubble wrap, giving a bubbly appearance to the diluted paint. Try using different-sized bubble pack to alter the effect.

Sponging off with a plastic bag.

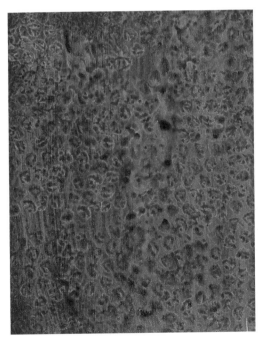

Sponging off with bubble wrap.

Dry brush work.

Distressed paint effect.

DRY BRUSH WORK

Dry brush work is easy and gives an interesting texture to a painted surface.

Begin by choosing a colour to contrast with your base coat. Place a little of the paint into a mixing dish and leave it to stand for 10 minutes to dry a little.

Use a household paintbrush with fairly long bristles and make sure that the brush is completely dry. Dip the tips of the bristles into the paint and then wipe the brush on to paper towelling until there is no paint left in the brush.

Holding the brush upright, skim the tips of the bristles over the base coat, thus brushing on very faint colour. Criss-cross the brush strokes to gradually build up the texture. Add more paint to the brush as it becomes necessary, but wipe the brush thoroughly after each new application of paint.

DISTRESSED PAINT EFFECT

This simple paint effect gives a worn, antique appearance to a project.

You will need to choose a colour to contrast quite sharply with the base coat. Begin by rubbing a little wax polish on to the areas of the base coat where you would like the worn effect to be. Ideally, it should be on the areas of your project where you would expect most wear and tear to occur, such as edges, handles, the lids of boxes, and so on.

The wax will resist the top layer of paint, making it easier to remove. Paint two coats of totally contrasting paint over the base coat, waxed areas included, and allow the paint to dry. When the paint has dried, take a piece of sandpaper and gently sand the parts of the project where wax was applied. This sandpapering will gradually reveal some of the base colour until it shows through the top layer of paint in an irregular way. This will resemble the appearance of much-weathered paintwork on boats and old buildings.

CHAPTER 8

Moon and Stars

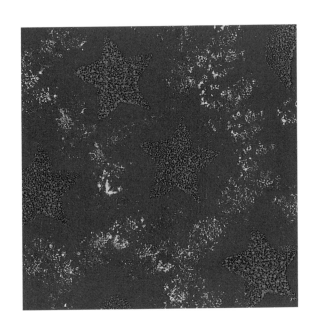

Moon and Stars

This little design is very easy to print and projects can be completed very quickly, satisfying even the most impatient of craft workers.

TOOLS AND MATERIALS
Basic equipment including two foam sponge pads

Additional Materials
A piece of natural sea sponge

Paint
Dark blue (ultramarine)
Bronze metallic acrylic paint
Gold metallic acrylic paint

METHOD
1 Prepare and prime your project as described in Chapter 2.

2 Paint your project with dark blue paint. Apply two or more coats to ensure that the priming paint is completely covered. Set aside to allow the paint to dry .

3 Prepare the printing blocks as described in Chapter 5. The circle and the crescent shape can both be cut from one sponge pad. When cutting the star motif from the second sponge pad, cut off the unwanted portion of the sponge and retain this portion for future use.

4 Study your project and decide roughly how your motifs will be positioned.

Group the stars are grouped together to form small constellations. The crescent and the circle shapes can then be placed randomly to fill in the remaining spaces.

If you are in doubt about the positioning of your design, cut shapes from scrap paper to represent the printed motifs. Attach the paper shapes to your project with small pieces of masking tape. Move these shapes around until you are happy with the positioning. Use a soft pencil to lightly mark the positions on the project and remove the paper shapes.

5 Using a watercolour brush, coat the star-shaped sponge block with bronze paint. Test print onto newspaper to blot any excess paint. Print the stars in their allocated positions. Vary the brightness of the stars by allowing some of the printing to become faint in places.

Apply more paint to the sponge if the printing becomes too faint, remembering to test print after every fresh application of paint.

6 Apply bronze paint to the crescent-shaped sponge and print this motif in the same way as before.

7 Repeat the process using the circular printing block, printing the circles to fill any remaining spaces. Allow the paint to dry thoroughly.

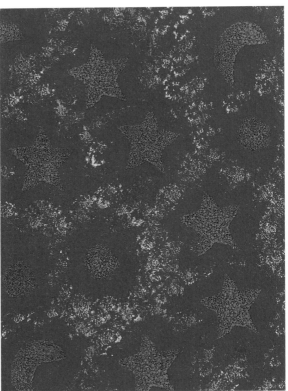

8 To complete the design, squeeze a small amount of gold metallic paint into a mixing dish. Dampen the piece of sea sponge and squeeze out any excess water. Dip the sponge into the gold paint and gently sponge a pattern of gold in the spaces around the bronze star motifs.

9 When the paint is thoroughly dry, apply varnish or wax to protect your work from wear and tear.

Further Ideas and Options
This design also works well with silver motifs painted on to a background of deep purple. The sponging would be equally effective using either silver or pearl white metallic paint.

An inexpensive and stylish makeover for a teenager's bedroom could be accomplished using this design. You can paint the furniture in dark blue with a band of the pattern painted on the drawer fronts, cupboard doors, and so on. Accessories can be decorated in mix-and-match style using plain dark blue paint, dark blue with gold sponging and plain bronze paint.

CHAPTER 9

Flowerpot Designs

Flowerpot Designs

Clay flowerpots are inexpensive and easily obtainable and therefore make excellent projects on which to practise new designs and colour combinations.

The designs illustrated have all been developed to help demonstrate how simple shapes can be used in different ways to create a variety of patterns.

These small projects provide an opportunity to practise many of the techniques used throughout the book.

1 Red Pot with Heart Design

TOOLS AND MATERIALS
Basic equipment including one half of a sponge pad

Additional Materials
Clay flowerpot

Paint
Scarlet
White

METHOD
1 Seal the flowerpot as described in Chapter 2.

2 Paint the pot with scarlet paint, applying two or more coats to ensure good coverage. Allow the paint to dry.

3 Using a household paintbrush, dry brush the rim of the pot with white paint. Follow the guidelines given for dry brushing on pages 21–22 in Chapter 7. Allow the paint to dry.

4 Using the heart-shaped template A on page 111, cut out the printing block as described in Chapter 5. Retain any small off-cuts of sponge to use later.

5 Coat the heart-shaped printing block with white paint and test print to blot excess paint.

6 Print the heart-shaped motifs randomly on the pot, turning each one so that the hearts face in different directions. Space the hearts evenly and do not overcrowd them. Set the pot aside to dry.

7 Apply several coats of varnish to waterproof the pot completely.

2 Trefoil Design

TOOLS AND MATERIALS
Basic equipment

Additional Materials
Sponge pad off-cuts
Clay flowerpot
Heart-shaped printing block cut from template A

Paint
Your own choice of colours

METHOD
1 Seal the flowerpot as described in Chapter 2.

2 Paint the flowerpot with the colour of your choice. Apply two or more coats, allowing the paint to dry between coats.

3 Coat the heart-shaped printing block with your choice of colour and test print onto newspaper.

4 Print three heart-shaped motifs, pointed ends together to form the cloverleaf. You could make some of the cloverleaves into the four-leaved, 'lucky' variety. Continue to print them, but positioned in different directions.

5 To paint the stems you will need to use a small off-cut of sponge. Cut a thin strip of sponge using template B as a guide. Coat the long thin edge of this strip of sponge with paint.

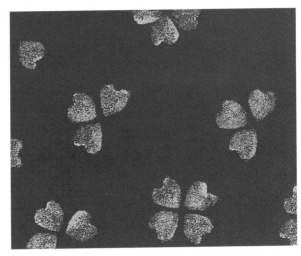

Hold the strip of sponge slightly curved between your finger and thumb and use to print a stem for each of your printed cloverleaves. Curve the stems in different directions for added interest.

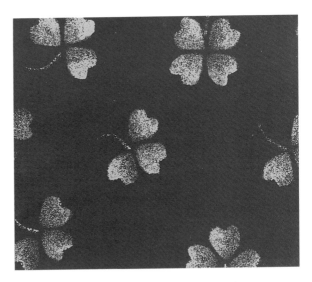

6 When your pot is dry, apply varnish to seal and protect your work.

3 Pale Blue Pot with Cloud Design

TOOLS AND MATERIALS
Basic equipment including one half of a sponge pad

Additional materials
Clay flowerpot
Natural sea sponge

Paint
Dark blue (ultramarine)
White
Black

METHOD
1 Seal the flowerpot as described in Chapter 2, by mixing a little varnish with water. Two coats af sealant will suffice for this project.

2 Mix a little dark blue paint into white to create pale blue. Paint the flowerpot with pale blue paint, applying two or more coats to ensure good, even coverage. Allow the paint to dry.

3 Prepare the cloud-shaped printing block using template C on page 111. Follow the guidelines given in Chapter 5. Retain any small off-cuts of sponge for later use.

4 Coat the cloud-shaped printing block with white paint and test print. Print the clouds on the blue background, grouping some closer together than others.

5 Add a few wispy clouds with a piece of natural sponge. Dampen the sponge and dip it into the white paint. Use the sponge to dab on an impression of wispy cloud formations between the larger clouds. Allow the paint to dry.

6 To paint the birds you will need to use a small off-cut of sponge. Cut a thin strip of sponge, using template D on page 111 as a guide.

7 Coat the edge of the strip of sponge with black paint. Hold the piece of sponge slightly curved between your finger and thumb. Before printing the birds on your project, practise a few on

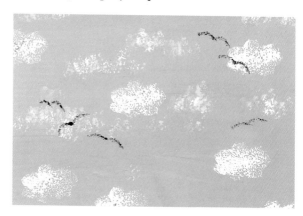

scrap paper or newspaper. Print two little curved lines, joined together, to represent a bird in flight. Vary the angle of the birds and print as many as you wish. Allow the paint to dry.

8 Complete your flowerpot by applying several coats of varnish.

4 Sheep Design

TOOLS AND MATERIALS
Basic equipment including one half of a sponge pad

Additional Materials
Printing blocks cut from templates C, D and E
Clay flowerpot

Paint
Background colour of your own choice
White
Black

METHOD
1 Seal the flowerpot as described in Chapter 2.

2 Paint the flowerpot in the colour of your choice. Add a paint effect in a contrasting colour if desired.

3 Coat the cloud-shaped printing block cut from template C with white paint and test print once or twice.

4 Print the bodies of the sheep, varying

the angle at which you place each one, to give a lively appearance to the work. Print as many sheep as you wish and then set the pot aside to dry.

5 Using template E from page 111, cut out the head-shaped printing block. Retain any small off-cuts of sponge to use later.

6 Coat the printing block with black paint and test print once or twice. Print a head for each sheep, placing the heads at different ends of the bodies so that the sheep are facing in different directions. Allow the paint to dry.

7 Using template D as a guide, cut a thin strip of sponge from one of the reserved off-cuts.

8 Coat the long edge of the strip of sponge with black paint and use it to print the sheep's legs. Print the legs slanting outwards to give the impression of movement. Allow the paint to dry.

9 Apply several coats of varnish to waterproof the pot completely.

5 Turquoise Pot with Flower Sprig Design

TOOLS AND MATERIALS
Basic equipment including one half of a sponge pad

Additional Materials
Clay flower pot and template F and G

Paint
Dark blue (ultramarine)
White
Bright yellow (cadmium yellow)
Scarlet

METHOD
1 Seal the flowerpot as described in Chapter 2.

2 To paint the background you will need to mix a turquoise-coloured paint. Mix dark blue into white to create a pale blue. In a separate dish, mix together bright yellow and dark blue paint to create a medium green colour. Add a little of the green paint to the pale blue, gradually adding more green if necessary until you have a pretty turquoise colour. Cover the dish of green paint with clingfilm and retain for later use.

Paint the flowerpot with turquoise paint, applying two or more coats to ensure good, even coverage. Allow the paint to dry.

3 For the dry brush paint effect you will need to mix a little yellow and a little scarlet paint into white to create a cream colour with just a hint of peach.

Follow the guidelines given in Chapter 7 for creating a dry brush paint effect. Use the peach-coloured paint to dry brush the flowerpot both inside and out. Allow the paint to dry.

4 To paint the flowers you will need to mix a deeper shade of peach. Add a little more bright yellow and scarlet paint to your original peachy cream colour and cover the dish of paint with clingfilm to prevent it drying out.

5 Cut out the flower-shaped printing block from template F on page 111.

6 Uncover the dish of peach paint and coat the flower printing block with this

colour. Add a small stroke of red paint to the pointed base of the flower shape (see the colour guide). Test print once or twice to blend the colours.

7 Print the flowers on the pot, spacing them irregularly and positioning them at different angles. Print as many as you wish and then leave the pot to dry.

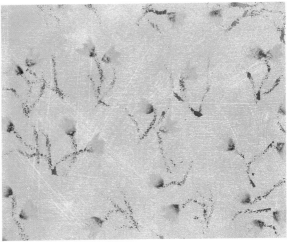

10 Complete your flowerpot by applying several coats of varnish.

6 Blue Pot with Flower Garland Design

TOOLS AND MATERIALS
Basic equipment

Additional Materials
Clay flowerpot
Sponge block cut from template F
Natural sea sponge

Paint
Dark blue (ultramarine)
White
Scarlet
Bright yellow (cadmium yellow)
Black

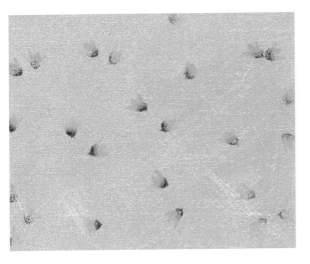

8 Using template G on page 111 as a guide, cut a thin strip of sponge to print the stems and leaves.

Use the green paint that you mixed earlier and coat the long thin edge of the strip of sponge.

9 Hold the strip of sponge slightly curved between your finger and thumb and print a stem for each flower. Curve the stems in different directions. Using the same piece of sponge, print a few spiky leaves beside each flower stem. Allow the paint to dry.

METHOD

1 Seal the flowerpot as described in Chapter 2.

2 Mix a small quantity of dark blue paint into white to create a pale shade of blue. Paint your flowerpot with pale blue paint applying two or more coats to give good, even coverage. Allow the paint to dry.

3 Follow the dry brushing guidelines given in Chapter 7. Use white paint to dry brush over the pale blue undercoat both inside the pot and out. Allow the paint to dry.

4 To sponge paint the leafy border you will need to use two shades of green. Use bright yellow and dark blue paint to mix a light, yellowish green and a deeper, bluish green.

Dampen a piece of sea sponge and dip it into your lighter green colour. Use the sponge to dab on a delicate tracery of foliage. Continue to sponge this green foliage in a broad band all the way around the pot.

While the paint is still wet, dip the sponge into the darker green paint and repeat the process, dabbing the darker coloured paint over the light. The two greens will blend together to create a subtle effect. Try to keep the sponging light and delicate to represent soft ferny foliage. Allow the paint to dry.

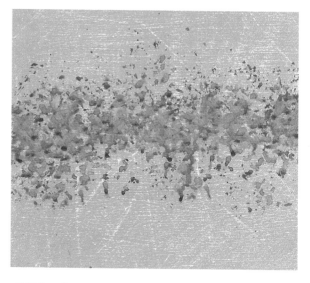

5 Take the sponge block cut from template F and coat with white paint. Add a stroke of scarlet paint to the pointed end of the printing block (see the colour guide). Test print once or twice to blend the two colours.

The printing block will form the four petals of a flower. Print the block four times with the pointed ends together in the centre. This will form a flower with a contrasting centre. Print all the flowers in the same way, allowing some of the printing to become faint in places.

While the paint is drying, wash and dry the printing block ready for the next stage of the design.

6 To print the flower buds, coat the printing block with white paint as before but add a contrast of green paint to the pointed tip (see the colour guide).

Print the buds between the open
flowers. Use the bud motif to fill in
spaces and to 'soften' the design.

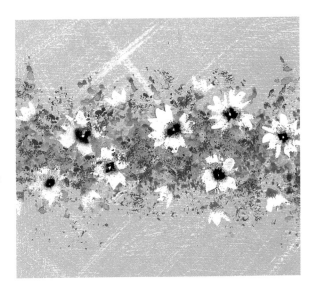

7 Use the natural sponge, dipped into
the dark green paint, to add more ferny
foliage overlapping some of the flowers.

8 Use a fine watercolour brush to paint a
tiny white dot in the centre of each open
flower. Allow the paint to dry.

9 Complete your flowerpot by applying
several coats of varnish.

Further Ideas and Options
Simple motifs, such as the heart shape,
could be mixed and matched with the
template shapes used in the Moon and
Stars project. Other geometric shapes
could be introduced to create many
intriguing patterns and designs.

An oval shape would make a pretty
cameo on which to overprint the flower
sprig motif. A checkerboard effect of
coloured squares could be overprinted
with stars, circles, hearts and so on.

Don't be afraid to experiment with a
range of colours, too. Often a simple
design looks stunningly different when
painted in another colour combination.

Finally, if you have a large flowerpot or
other suitable project, try printing the
sheep motif on a background of green,
sponged grass. Use a piece of natural
sponge to paint bushes and trees. Add a
cloud-filled bright blue sky up above
and you will have built up a realistic
little rural scene.

CHAPTER 10

Leaves and Cherries

Leaves and Cherries

The aim of this design of leaves and cherries is to create a country kitchen style. The distressed paintwork in green and cream gives a homely appearance to the projects.

Two different-sized templates (see page 112) have been provided to increase the flexibility of the design. Using these two templates, you can decorate a delightful range of matching kitchen accessories.

TOOLS AND MATERIALS
Basic equipment including a sponge pad

Additional Materials
Wax polish
Sandpaper

Paint
Cream
Dark blue (ultramarine)
Bright yellow (cadmium yellow)
Scarlet
White
Black

METHOD
1 Prepare and prime your project as described in Chapter 2.

2 To paint the undercoat you will need to mix a dark green colour. Mix bright yellow paint and dark blue paint together and add a little black. Add more black paint if necessary to create a dark forest green.

3 Paint your primed project with the green paint. Apply two coats of paint, allowing the paint to dry thoroughly between coats.

4 Follow the guidelines for the distressed paint effect given in Chapter 7 and apply wax polish to your project.

5 Paint over the whole project with cream paint. You will need to apply several coats of paint to cover the dark green undercoat completely. Allow the paint to dry thoroughly.

6 Use a small piece of sandpaper gently to rub away some of the cream paint on the areas where wax was applied. Reveal as much or as little of the green undercoat as you wish.

7 Prepare the printing blocks as described in Chapter 5.

8 To paint the cherry leaves you will need to mix two shades of green. Mix bright yellow and dark blue paint together to create a medium green shade. In a separate dish, mix a second quantity of this medium green colour

and add a little white paint to create a lighter shade of green.

9 Coat the leaf printing block with the light green paint and add a contrast of darker green to one half of the leaf (see the colour guide). Test print once or twice to blend the two colours and blot any excess paint.

At this stage it is a good idea to test out the design before beginning to print on your project. Practise printing the leaves until you feel confident enough to work on your project.

10 Print the leaves one by one, grouping them into a fan shape. Keep the printing of these first leaves fairly light in texture. Allow the paint to dry.

11 Coat the sponge printing block with the same colours you used before and test print.

Print a group of five leaves, placed centrally and just below the previous printing. These five leaves need to be slightly heavier in paint than the initial printing. If they do not look heavy enough to provide the necessary contrast, then print again over the top of the original imprint. When you are satisfied with this part of the design, set the project aside to dry.

12 To paint the cherries you will need to mix a deep red paint. Add a small amount of dark blue paint to scarlet to create a rich crimson red.

13 Coat the cherry printing block with the deep red paint. Use a fine watercolour brush to add a tiny white dot for the highlight (see the colour guide). Test print once or twice. You may need to renew the white highlight after each imprint, because the paint is quickly absorbed into the darker colour.

Print two or three cherries just below the printed leaves.

14 Mix a little brown paint by adding scarlet to your original medium green leaf colour. Use the brown paint and a fine watercolour brush to paint in the cherry stalks.

15 To soften the design and give a little more depth of field to the work, use the leaf-shaped printing block very dry of paint to sponge in a very light impression of leaves in the background of the work. Allow the paint to dry thoroughly.

16 Complete your project by applying wax or varnish.

If you would like to expand the design into a more dramatic one depicting large bunches of cherries, follow the same guidelines but print with a heavier texture of paint. Add a further layer of leaves overlapping some of the fruits and again using a heavier texture of paint.

Further Ideas and Options

If you prefer a more sophisticated background to the cherry design, the cream metallic finish described in Chapter 11 works very well. Accessories for the dining table, a wine cooler or fruit bowl could also be decorated in this way.

The basic construction of a fan-shaped arrangement of leaves makes a suitable background for any small flower motif.

Remember that flowers need not always be realistically represented; they can be made more abstract and symbolic. Why not experiment with some fanciful designs and colour schemes of your own for other projects?

If, however, you do prefer to use a realistic image, then gardening books, seed and plant catalogues and real-life gardens can provide a rich source of ideas and inspiration.

CHAPTER 11

Christmas Design

Christmas Design

Christmas projects are fun to produce and if given as gifts they are usually much appreciated. This festive design of holly and mistletoe may appear a little complicated, but it is not at all difficult to print.

I have chosen to decorate very inexpensive items: a metal tray for serving drinks and two little wooden dishes to hold nuts and sweets.

Christmas parties provide an excellent opportunity to display your creative handiwork, but be prepared – many of your guests will ask you to decorate similar items for them!

TOOLS AND MATERIALS
Basic equipment including two foam sponge pads

Paint
Cream
Champagne metallic acrylic paint
Emerald green metallic acrylic paint
Pearl white metallic acrylic paint
Scarlet
Dark blue (ultramarine)
Bright yellow (cadmium yellow)
Black
White

METHOD
1 Prepare and prime your project as described in Chapter 2.

2 Paint your project with cream paint, applying two or more coats to cover the priming paint completely. Allow the paint to dry.

3 You will need to follow the guidelines for the sponging off method described in Chapter 7. Paint the project with champagne metallic paint and then use a ball of crumpled kitchen paper to sponge a texture into the paint. Allow to dry.

4 Prepare leaves as separate blocks. This will enable you to print the leaves in pairs but spaced at slightly different angles, thus avoiding too regular and uniform an arrangement.

5 To paint the mistletoe leaves you will need to mix a light greyish green colour. Begin by mixing bright yellow, dark blue and white paint together to create a very pale green. Add a tiny amount of black paint to give a grey tinge to the green colour. Coat the two mistletoe printing blocks with pale green paint and test print several times.

6 Print the mistletoe leaves in pairs and facing outwards to form the outside edge of your design. Follow the shape of your project, that is, circular, oblong or whatever, when printing this border.

Cover the dish of pale green paint for later and set the project aside to dry.

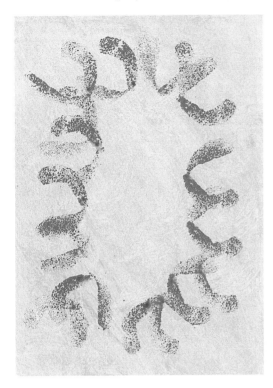

7 To paint the first holly leaves you will need to mix a dark green coloured paint. Mix bright yellow and dark blue paint together and add a little black to darken the colour.

Coat the smallest holly leaf printing blocks with dark green paint and test print the design.

8 Print the holly leaves pointing outwards from the centre of the design towards the mistletoe border. Keep the spacing irregular and print some of the leaves joined together in pairs. Allow the paint to dry.

9 Coat the second holly leaf printing block with dark green paint and add a contrast of emerald green metallic paint to one half of the leaf (see the colour guide). Test print to blend the two colours to best effect.

10 Print the brighter green holly leaves randomly to fill the spaces within the design. Overlap some of the dark leaves and some of the mistletoe border. Allow the paint to dry.

11 Coat the smaller berry printing block with scarlet paint. Use a fine watercolour brush to add a tiny white dot on the berry to represent a shiny highlight (see the colour guide). Test

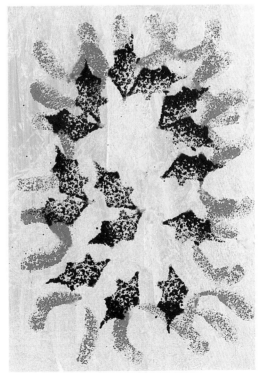

design. Add a few more berries between the pairs of mistletoe leaves on the outside border of the design.

15 Complete your project by applying several coats of varnish.

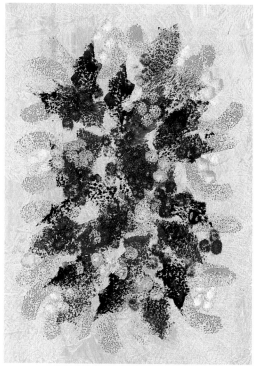

print to blot excess paint. You will find that you need to renew the highlight quite frequently because the light colour will be quickly absorbed into the dark.

12 Print the holly berries in small groups, allowing the printing to become quite faint in some areas. Allow the paint to dry.

13 Coat the larger berry printing block with white metallic paint. Uncover the dish of greyish green paint and use it to paint a thin green line round the outside edge of the berry (see the colour guide).

14 Print the mistletoe berries in small groups within the main body of the

Further Ideas and Options
Many of the images popularly associated with Christmas would make excellent subjects for sponge painted designs. Bells, baubles, candles, snow-covered spruce trees, could all provide design ideas for painting Christmas projects.

Plants such as the poinsettia, Christmas rose and solanum (the little winter cherry with bright orange berries) could all be used to create further festive designs.

The Christmas season is a good excuse for over indulging in metallic colours. Gold, silver and bronze could be used as background foils to designs of brightly coloured stars and baubles.

A roll of wallpaper lining paper (or indeed, any other paper) decorated with any of these motifs would make a unique and inexpensive giftwrap. Home-made gift tags, made from cut-out card and decorated to match, could complete impressive 'designer look' Christmas parcels.

CHAPTER 12

Climbing Ivy

Climbing Ivy

This design featuring climbing stems of ivy is an obvious choice for decorating picture or mirror frames.

Tools and Materials
Basic equipment including one and a half sponge pads

Paint
Terracotta
Cream
White
Bright yellow (cadmium yellow)
Dark blue (ultramarine)
Black

Method
1 Prepare and prime your project as described in Chapter 2.

2 Paint your project with terracotta paint, applying two or more coats to ensure good even coverage. Allow the paint to dry.

3 Prepare the printing blocks as described in Chapter 5. You will need to cut three blocks using templates A, B and C on page 113. Reserve any small off-cuts of sponge to use later.
4 Study your project and decide roughly how your leaves will be placed. At this

stage you may find it helpful to make a rough sketch of your design. Although this design appears to be very simple in construction, the spacing of the leaves and the angles at which they are placed need to be considered carefully to give a balanced and attractive appearance to the work. Use a pencil lightly to mark your project with the proposed positions of the leaves.

5 To paint the leaves you will need to mix two shades of green. Mix bright yellow and dark blue paint together to create a medium shade of green. In a separate dish mix a small quantity of the same colour and add a tiny amount of black paint to darken the colour slightly.

6 Coat the printing block cut from template A with cream paint. Use a fine watercolour brush to put a little white paint on the very edges of the leaf. Add a contrast of medium green to the centre of the leaf and then add a further contrast of dark green paint (see the colour guide). Test print several times to blot excess paint and blend the colours.

7 Using a very light pressure on the sponge, print the background leaves at irregular intervals and varying angles. Remember to leave enough space at the top of the work to print smaller leaves later. Allow the paint to dry.

8 Coat the same printing block with the same colours as before and test print.

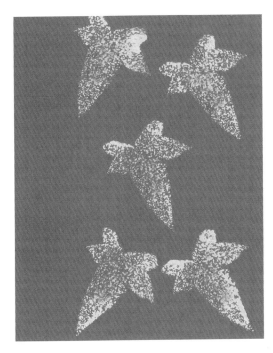

9 Print the foreground leaves overlapping some of the previous printing. Apply heavier pressure on the sponge to give a much stronger definition to this second group of leaves. Allow the paint to dry.

10 Coat the printing block cut from template B with cream paint. Use a fine watercolour brush to add a contrast of

medium green paint to the centre of the leaf (see the colour guide). Test print to blot excess paint.

11 Print two or three of these smaller leaves at the top of your climbing stem. Allow the paint to dry.

12 Coat the printing block cut from template C with cream paint and test print until the printing becomes faint.

13 Print this little motif at the top of the stem to represent unfurling leaves.

14 To print the stems you will need to cut a very thin strip of sponge to use as a printing block. Use template D as a guide to cut this from a sponge off-cut.

15 Coat the long thin edge of the strip of foam with medium green paint. Hold the strip of sponge slightly curved between finger and thumb and print a few small lines between some of the leaves. This should give you just a suggestion of stems amongst the leaves and should not be too heavy or too pronounced.

16 Take the printing block cut from template E and coat it with cream paint. Test print until you have removed most of the paint. Using a very light pressure on the sponge, add faint images of leaves in the background of the design. Be quite sparing with these images, using them to fill in any spaces and to give a little more depth to the design.

17 When your project is thoroughly dry, apply varnish or wax polish to seal and protect your work. The mirror frame shown in this project has been sealed with wax polish and buffed up to achieve a soft shine.

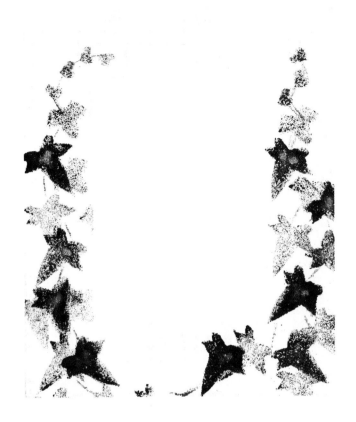

Further Ideas and Options
Extra ivy leaf templates have been provided to enable you to create different designs of your own. Winding stems of ivy painted in dark, subdued shades of green against a white background would make an attractive frame for a botanical print or a black and white photograph.

In addition, the ivy leaf design can be successfully painted as a horizontal band to frame projects of various shapes, for example a pair of lamp shades for the bedroom, a photo album or, if laminated, place mats for the dining room table. Greater flexibility can be achieved by using only the smallest leaves to decorate a tiny project.

Finally, if you have access to suitable plant material, try using real leaves from your own garden as templates. Draw around the leaf directly on to a sponge pad to create a wonderfully accurate printing block.

CHAPTER 13

Flowers and Bees

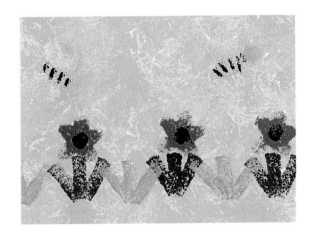

Flowers and Bees

This cheerful design featuring marigolds and bumblebees makes an amusing decoration for use in a playroom or child's bedroom.

The bumblebees have a friendly appearance, but if you feel that your child would prefer an insect without a sting in its tail, you could substitute the butterfly motif from Chapter 16 (see page 76).

TOOLS AND MATERIALS
Basic equipment including two foam sponge pads

Paint
Dark blue (ultramarine)
Scarlet
Bright yellow (cadmium yellow)
White
Pearl white metallic acrylic paint

METHOD
1 Prepare and prime your project as described in Chapter 2.

2 Mix white and dark blue paint together to create a mid-blue for the background of the design. In a separate dish, mix yellow and dark blue paint to create a mid-green shade. Add a little of the green paint to the blue, gradually adding more green if necessary until you have a bright shade of turquoise. Cover the dish of green paint with clingfilm and retain for use later.

3 Paint your project with the turquoise blue paint, applying two or more coats to ensure good coverage. Reserve any leftover paint, covered with clingfilm, and allow your project to dry thoroughly.

4 For the sponged paint effect you will need to mix a lighter shade of turquoise. Add a little white paint to your original colour to create a shade of blue that is a few tones lighter than your base coat.

5 Follow the guidelines given in Chapter 7 for the sponging on method. Use a ball of crumpled kitchen paper to sponge a random pattern of light turquoise paint over the darker base coat. Allow to dry.

6 Prepare the printing blocks as described in Chapter 5. Retain the off-cuts of sponge to use later.

7 You will need to measure your project to space the flower motifs evenly. The example shown places the dark green stems at 6cm (2⅜in) apart. If you are decorating a circular object such as the wastepaper bin or perhaps a lamp shade, you will need to refer to the

guidelines in Chapter 4, which describes the easiest way to measure a circular or other irregular object.

When adapting the design for a flat circular surface such as the stool top illustrated, you will need to measure in a different way, although it is quite straightforward. Place your stool upside-down on a piece of paper and use a pencil to draw around the outer edge of the stool. Cut out the outlined paper circle. Fold the piece of paper in half and in half again to form a quarter of the circle. Open out the paper and place on the stool top. Use the creased fold lines on the paper to mark quarter

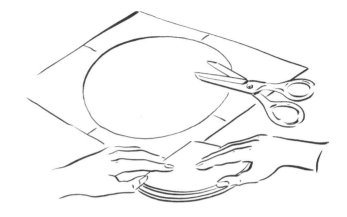

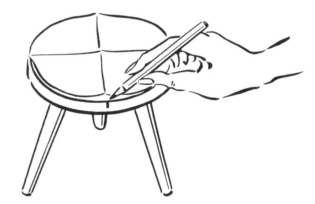

segments on the stool top. A dark green flower stem can then be placed on each quarter line and the lighter green flower stems and leaves can be placed in-between. Using very little pressure, mark with a pencil the positions of the flower stems.

To print the stems and leaves you will need two shades of green paint. Use the green paint that you set aside. Use this to paint the darker stems and leaves. To mix a lighter green colour, mix bright yellow and dark blue paint to create a yellowish green.

9 Coat the printing block cut from template A on page 113 with dark green paint and test print once or twice onto newspaper. Print a vertical green stem on each of your marked positions. With the same printing block, add the leaves that slant outwards from the base of each stem.

10 Wash and dry the printing block and coat it with the lighter green paint. Test print once or twice. Print the light green plants between the darker ones. Allow the paint to dry.

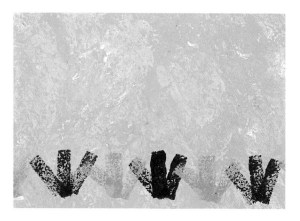

11 You will need to mix a bright orange colour with which to paint the marigold flowers. Mix together bright yellow and scarlet to achieve a vivid orange.

12 Coat the printing block cut from template B on page 113 with orange paint and test print once or twice. Print a flower head at the top of each dark green stem.

13 To paint the bees you will need to mix a golden yellow colour. Mix a tiny

amount of scarlet red paint into bright yellow to achieve a warm, happy colour.

14 Coat the printing block cut from template C on page 113 with golden yellow paint. Print the bees at varying angles as though they are hovering just above the flowers. Allow the paint to dry thoroughly.

15 To paint the flower centres and the stripes on the bees, mix a dark brown. Begin by mixing bright yellow and dark blue paint together to create a medium green. Add scarlet paint to the green and blend thoroughly to achieve a warm dark brown shade.

16 Coat the printing block cut from template D on page 113 with dark brown paint and print a circle in the centre of each flower.

17 Using template shape E as a guide, cut a thin strip of sponge from one of the off-cuts reserved earlier.

18 Coat the thin edge of the strip of

sponge with brown paint. Hold the little strip of sponge slightly curved between your finger and thumb and print the stripes on the body of each bee. Allow the paint to dry.

19 To paint the bees' wings you will need to use the printing block cut from template F. Coat the sponge block with pearl white metallic paint and test print. Print a pair of overlapping wings on each side of each bee. Vary the position of the wings as shown in the illustration. Allow the paint to dry thoroughly.

20 Apply wax or varnish to complete your project.

Further Ideas and Options
This little design of flowers and bees would make an attractive border decoration for a child's room. The walls could be sponged with the same two shades of turquoise and the design painted directly on to the walls. Instead of placing the flowers in a row, you could form them as a series of random undulations. This would give a softer appearance to the design. For a small child, a design like this is best placed at the child's eye level or just below, rather than way above his or her head. You can achieve a co-ordinated look by using textile paints to print a matching fabric for other items: curtains, floor cushions,

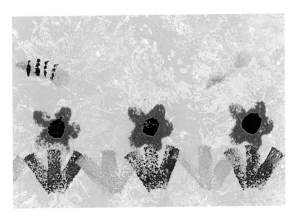

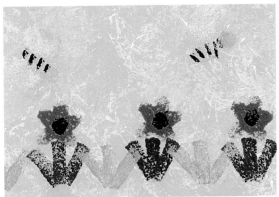

pyjama bags and so on. When designing for young children, simple shapes and bright colours are fundamental and sponge painting is admirably suited to this purpose.

Brightly coloured birds, insects and sea creatures will offer suitable images to interpret in this way.

If seeking ideas for basic animal shapes or other similar motifs, then children's picture books may provide inspiration.

Bread
Butter

CHAPTER 14

Sunflowers

Sunflowers

This sunflower design can easily be adapted to decorate a variety of projects. A single motif of one flower head backed by a few leaves makes a bold statement, or the design can be expanded to include as many flowers as you wish.

TOOLS AND MATERIALS
Basic equipment including two foam sponge pads

Paint
Dark blue (ultramarine)
Scarlet
Bright yellow (cadmium yellow)
Black
White

METHOD
1 Prepare and prime your project as described in Chapter 2.

2 Paint your project with dark blue paint, applying two or more coats to ensure good, even coverage. Allow the paint to dry.

3 For the sponged paint effect you will need a darker shade of blue than the base coat. Place dark blue paint in a mixing dish and blend a little black to create a dusky, very dark shade of blue.

Following the guidelines for the sponging on method given in Chapter 7,

apply splodges of the dark blue paint evenly over the base coat. Allow the paint to dry thoroughly.

4 Prepare the printing blocks as described in Chapter 5.

5 Before you begin to paint, decide where you wish your sunflowers to be placed. If in doubt, cut circles of scrap paper approximately 10cm (4in) in diameter and use these as a guide to represent the flower shapes. Use pieces of masking tape to stick the paper circles on to your project, moving the shapes around until you are happy with the positioning. Flowers can overlap, but take care not to overcrowd the design.

Use a pencil lightly to mark the position of the flowers on your project and then remove the paper circles.

6 You will need to mix two shades of green paint for the leaves. Mix together bright yellow and dark blue paint and then add a little white to this mixture. If the shade of green you have mixed

appears to be too dark or too bright, add a little more white paint. The aim is to mix a soft, fresh green shade.

Now transfer a small amount of the green paint to a separate dish. Add a little black paint to this to create a darker, greyish green to use for the shading of your leaves.

7 Coat the leaf-shaped printing block with light green paint. Using a fine watercolour brush, add a stroke of dark green paint slightly to one side of the centre of the leaf (see the colour guide). Test print once or twice to blend the colours and blot excess paint.

8 Print the leaves onto your project, grouping them around the marked positions for the flower heads. Add more paint to the sponge when the printing becomes too faint, but remember that a variety of textures make the design more effective than a uniform, solid mass of colour. When you have completed all your leaves set the project aside to allow the paint to dry.

9 To paint the sunflower centres, you will need to mix a dark brown colour. Use bright yellow and dark blue paint to create a medium shade of green. Add a roughly equal amount of scarlet paint to the green and mix them together thoroughly. If the colour appears greenish, add a little more scarlet paint. If the colour does not appear to be dark enough, add a little black paint.

10 Coat the circular printing block with dark brown paint. For the highlight, use a fine watercolour brush to paint a

white ring in the centre of the circular sponge (see the colour guide). Test print on to newspaper to blend the colours.

11 Print one brown circle in the centre of each marked flower position. Allow the paint to dry.

12 Coat the petal-shaped printing block with bright yellow paint and test print. Print the sunflower petals one by one, radiating outwards from the brown centre circle. Allow the paint to become fairly faint in places before re-coating the sponge. To give variety of colour, paint a little scarlet paint on the outside tip of the

petal-shaped printing block (see the colour guide). Test print on newspaper. The red colour should blend into the yellow to give an orange tinge to the ends of the petals. Work all the flower heads in the same way, adding more colour to the sponge as necessary. Allow to dry.

13 To complete the design you will need to print a few brighter coloured leaves, overlapping some of the flower heads. Mix bright yellow and dark blue paint together to create a bright green shade

and coat the leaf-shaped printing block. Test print once or twice.

14 Print a few of these brighter leaves so that they overlap some of the original leaves and some of the flower petals. This final layer of printing will give an illusion of depth to the design. Allow the paint to dry.

15 Apply one or two coats of wax or varnish to complete your project and allow it to dry thoroughly.

Further Ideas and Options

If you would like to experiment with the sunflowers against a different coloured background, don't be afraid to go ahead and try out your ideas. A background paint in two shades of deep green would work well, or you could use a rich deep red colour to give the work a Mediterranean feel.

Alterations to the basic design can be made to create an image of white daisies with yellow centres. You would need to cut a smaller circular printing block for the centre of the daisies to give them a dainty appearance. This daisy design would work well against a pale blue or pale green background.

If you begin to think of all the varieties of plants that produce daisy-type flowers you will be able to see possibilities for further designs and colour combinations.

Asters, dahlias, cosmos and many others could all be interpreted in a similar way.

CHAPTER 15

Vine Design

Vine Design

The use of metallic paints gives this design a luminous quality, representing the effect of sunlight filtering through the vine leaves.

This design provides ample opportunity for you to experiment with the use of colour to create a painted project, which will reflect your own style and individuality.

The tray and wine cooler would be perfect to use in an outdoor setting on a warm summer evening.

TOOLS AND MATERIALS
Basic equipment including two foam sponge pads

Paint
Dark blue (ultramarine)
Bright yellow (cadmium yellow)
Scarlet
White
Black
Cream
Bronze metallic acrylic paint
Amethyst metallic acrylic paint
Pearl white metallic acrylic paint

METHOD
1 Prepare and prime your project as described in Chapter 2.

2 For the background colour, mix a very pale shade of green. Combine dark blue and bright yellow paint with white to create this colour. Paint your project with the pale green, applying two or more coats to cover the priming paint. Allow the paint to dry.

3 For the sponged paint effect you will need to use the bronze metallic paint and employ the sponging off method. Paint a watery mixture of bronze paint over the green base coat. Use a ball of crumpled kitchen paper to sponge off some of the bronze colour, allowing the green base coat to show through in a random pattern. Allow the paint to dry.

4 Prepare the printing blocks as described in Chapter 5.

5 The first layer of printed leaves needs to be painted in dark shades of green. Use bright yellow and dark blue paint, plus black, to achieve a dark green. Now experiment with the same three colours, using them in different proportions to mix a variety of dark shades of green.

6 Coat the leaf-shaped printing block with dark green paint and add contrasts of slightly lighter and darker shades. Test print to check the colouring and adjust the colour if necessary.

7 Print the first layer of leaves onto your project, adding new colours to the printing block after making each imprint. Allow the paint to dry thoroughly.

8 You will need to mix a dark purple colour to paint the grapes. Mix together dark blue and scarlet paint to achieve a deep purple colour.

9 Coat the grape-shaped printing block with purple paint and do a test print.

10 Print the first layer of grapes, positioning them to form a roughly triangular shape. Print some of the grapes at the outside edge of the bunch with a lighter pressure than those in the centre. This will help to give an illusion of depth to the finished design. Allow the paint to dry.

11 Coat the grape printing block with amethyst metallic paint. Test print to blot excess paint, then apply over the paint already on the sponge.

12 Print a second layer of grapes in the centre of the bunch only. The shiny nature of these amethyst-painted grapes will create a realistic three-dimensional effect. Allow the paint to dry.

13 Coat the grape-shaped printing block with pearl white metallic paint, again applying the paint over the colour already in the sponge. Test print once or twice to allow the colours to blend.

14 Print a very few of these lighter coloured grapes, placed in the very centre of the bunch only. Allow the paint to dry.

15 Use dark blue, bright yellow, cream and white paint to create four or five different shades of light green. Now you can experiment freely with these colours to print a second layer of leaves onto your project.

16 Coat the leaf-shaped printing block with light green paint and add contrasts of lighter and darker shades of green. When you have added contrasting colours to the sponge, test print each time to check the effect of the colouring and that you like the way the colours blend together.

17 Print as many leaves as you wish, adding new colours to the sponge after making each imprint. Position some of the leaves to overlap the grapes slightly. Allow the paint to dry.

You can achieve a slightly different texture by painting the leaves in light shades of green and allowing the paint to dry before printing over the top with darker colours. Keep the printing block fairly dry of paint and overprint lightly for as delicate an effect as possible. It can be tricky to align the printing block but don't worry, it does not have to be exactly positioned to be effective. Indeed, it should not be too perfect.

18 If you wish to add twigs and stems, you can either use a fine paintbrush to apply the paint, or print them with a thin strip of sponge as a printing block. When you have completed your project, allow the paint to dry thoroughly.

19 Apply several coats of wax or varnish to protect your work.

Further Ideas and Options

This design would be look completely different, but equally effective, if green grapes were painted against a dark-coloured background. Again, metallic paints could be used to give an illusion of depth to the design.

A simplified colour scheme and a reduction in size would give you a motif to use for decorating kitchen accessories or a wall. A fake tile effect could be accomplished by painting small bunches of grapes inside coloured squares outlined with shadow.

CHAPTER 16

Bamboo and Butterflies

Bamboo and Butterflies

Extreme simplicity of form and a restrained use of colour give this design an Oriental appearance, making it perfect for the pair of Japanese-style vases illustrated.

The unobtrusiveness of this design depicting bamboo and orange-tip butterflies ensures that it will blend with every style of décor.

TOOLS AND MATERIALS
Basic equipment including two foam sponge pads

Additional Materials
Thin plastic bag

Paint
White
Dark blue (ultramarine)
Bright yellow (cadmium yellow)
Black
Scarlet
Pearl white metallic acrylic paint

METHOD
1 Prepare and prime your project as described in Chapter 2.

2 You will need to mix a pale blue-green colour with which to paint the background of the design. Combine white paint with a little yellow and a slightly larger proportion of dark blue to achieve this light colour. Paint your project with pale green paint, applying two or more coats to ensure good, even coverage. Allow the paint to dry.

3 For the sponged paint effect, you will need to employ the sponging off method, using a crumpled plastic bag. Brush a watery mixture of pearl white metallic paint over the green base coat. Use the crumpled plastic bag to dab over the painted surface, creating a mottled pattern in the white paint. Allow the paint to dry.

4 Prepare the printing blocks as described in Chapter 5.

5 The bamboo leaves are painted in muted shades of blue-green and grey-green. You will need to experiment with blending together white, black, blue and yellow paint to create these shades.

6 Coat the leaf-shaped printing block cut from template A on page 115 with a light, blue-green colour. Test print several times to remove excess paint.

7 Using a very light pressure on the sponge, print the first layer of leaves in upright sprays as illustrated. The topmost pair of leaves on each spray

should form the 'V' shape characteristic of bamboo. Allow the paint to dry.

8 The second layer of leaves needs to be printed with many of the leaves sloping towards the left. This will give the impression of being blown by the wind into graceful movement.

You will need to use both leaf-shaped printing blocks and the variety of light green shades of paint that you mixed earlier. One by one, add the different colours to the sponges to give subtle changes of colour and highlights of light and dark.

9 Print as many leaves as you wish but avoid overcrowding the design. Leave some spaces between the stems of bamboo to help keep the effect light, airy and with an oriental 'feel' about it. Allow the paint to dry.

10 You will need to mix a small amount of bright orange paint for the wing tips of the butterflies. Combine yellow and scarlet paint and add a little white to lighten the colour. You will also need dark brown paint for the wing tips and the bodies of the butterflies. Combine green and scarlet paint to create a reddish brown colour.

11 Coat the butterfly-shaped printing block with white paint and add orange and brown to the wing tips as indicated in the colour guide. Use a fine watercolour brush to add these colours to the sponge. Do a test print. (You may need to renew the contrasting colours frequently if the colours disappear.)

12 Print the butterflies, placing them

sparingly to maintain the simplicity of the design. Allow the paint to dry.

13 Coat the butterfly body printing block with brown paint and test print to remove excess paint.

14 Print a brown body in the centre of each of your butterflies. Set the project aside to allow the paint to dry thoroughly.

15 Apply wax or varnish to complete your project.

Further Ideas and Options

The bamboo design is so flexible that it can easily be adapted to decorate many different projects. You can decorate a tall, thin vase with a single graceful stem, or a large folding screen for your living room with a forest of stems.

Stems of bamboo could be incorporated into a design featuring some of the flowers often associated with Oriental art, such as peonies, chrysanthemums and sprigs of flowering cherry. They could be grouped together to create a beautiful composite design.

CHAPTER 17

Clematis Design

Clematis Design

This design features the variety of clematis named 'Nelly Moser', a plant much loved by gardeners for its prolific pink and white flowers. Reproduced in paint, the almost fairy-tale prettiness of these flowers can be enjoyed all year round.

The photograph shows the design painted as a broad band encircling the projects. You may prefer to completely cover your project with a profusion of flowers and foliage.

TOOLS AND MATERIALS
Basic equipment including two foam sponge pads

Additional Materials
Natural sea sponge

Paint
White
Black
Scarlet
Dark blue (ultramarine)
Bright yellow (cadmium yellow)

METHOD
1 Prepare and prime your project as described in Chapter 2.

2 To paint the background for the design you will need to mix a mid-grey colour. Combine white paint with a little black to achieve this medium shade of grey.

3 Paint your project with the grey paint, applying two or more coats to cover the priming paint. Allow the paint to dry.

4 For the sponged paint effect you will need to mix a lighter shade of grey. Combine white paint with a very small proportion of black to achieve this pale shade of grey.

5 Use a piece of natural sea sponge and the sponging on method to apply the pale grey paint in an even pattern of splodges all over the base coat. When you have completed this sponging, set the project aside to dry.

6 Prepare the printing blocks as described in Chapter 5.

7 To paint the background leaves you will need to mix both a light and a dark shade of green. Combine bright yellow and dark blue paint in different proportions to mix these shades. Add a little black paint to the darker green to dull the colour slightly.

8 Coat the largest of the leaf-shaped printing blocks with dark green paint. If

you wish, add a contrast of light green.

9 Print the dark green leaves, in groups of three, as shown in the illustration.

10 Coat the smaller leaf-shaped printing block with light green paint. If you wish, add a highlight of dark green.

11 Print the light green leaves, positioned in groups of three, as shown in the illustration. Allow to dry.

12 Before beginning the next step, you will find it helpful to refer to the guidelines given in the flower garland project (see page 36), which explains the method used to sponge paint an impression of foliage.

Use dark green, then light green paint to sponge a delicate band of foliage between and slightly overlapping the printed leaves. Allow the paint to dry.

13 To print the flowers, begin by coating the petal-shaped printing block with white paint. Mix a little scarlet paint into white to create a bright pink. Use a fine watercolour brush to add a pink stripe in the centre of the petal-shaped printing block (see the colour guide). Do a test print to blend the colours. (You will need to renew the pink stripe quite frequently, as the pink paint will be quickly absorbed into the white.)

14 To form each flower, print six petals in a circle with the pointed ends of the petals meeting in the centre. Align the petals as carefully as possible to ensure that they are evenly spaced. Continue until you have printed as many flowers as you wish. Allow the paint to dry.

15 To print the buds, coat the printing block with white paint and add a small amount of contrasting light green (see the colour guide).

16 Print the buds on the outer border of the design with the printed tips facing outwards. Slant the buds so that they face in different directions. Allow the paint to dry.

17 To print the flower centres you will need to coat the little circular printing block with light green paint. Use a fine brush to add a dot of bright yellow paint to the centre of the circle (see the colour guide).

18 Print a green centre for each flower, renewing the yellow dot if the colour becomes indistinct.

19 Finish the design by using the sea sponge to add a little more foliage between, and overlapping, some of the flowers and buds. Finally, dip the sea sponge into white paint and dab a delicate tracery of white over the green sponging and extending just beyond the border of the design. Allow the paint to dry thoroughly.

20 Apply wax or varnish to your project to protect your work.

Further Ideas and Options

It is usually helpful to observe directly from nature when planning a design based upon plants.

The extensive colour range of the different varieties of clematis could provide ideas for a wealth of stunning colour combinations. Close inspection of plant material can often reveal previously unnoticed characteristics. Reproducing the faded colours that have been exposed to strong sunlight and the differing number of petals borne by different varieties of the same plant will help to create a very realistic design.

Of course it is not always necessary to represent such flowers in a naturalistic way. The simple form of flowers such as clematis can easily be stylized and painted in unusual colours. Why not try some combinations of contemporary designs and colours?

Peaches

Strong colours and a heavy application of paint give this composition
its dramatic appeal. Layers of colour are built up to give texture and
depth to the design of peaches nestling amongst abundant foliage.

TOOLS AND MATERIALS
Basic equipment including two foam
sponge pads

Additional Materials
Natural sea sponge

Paint
Dark blue (ultramarine)
Bright yellow (cadmium yellow)
Scarlet
White
Black

METHOD
1 Prepare and prime your project as
described in Chapter 2.

2 To paint the base coat you will need to
mix a dark green colour. Combine dark
blue and bright yellow paint to create a
deep blue-green colour. Mix plenty,
because you'll need some for step 3.
Paint your project with the green paint,
applying two or more coats to cover the
priming paint completely. Allow the
paint to dry.

3 For the sponged paint effect you will
need to mix a shade of green slightly
darker than the base coat. Add a little
black paint to your blue-green colour to
produce a very dark, dusky green.

4 Using a piece of sea sponge and the
sponging on method, apply a dense
pattern of dark green paint all over the
base coat. Allow to dry.

5 Prepare the printing blocks as
described in Chapter 5.

6 To paint the first spray of leaves you
will need to mix a very pale green
colour. Combine bright yellow and dark
blue with white paint to create this light
shade. Use a larger proportion of dark
blue paint than yellow to give a striking
bluish shade of pale green.

7 Coat the leaf-shaped printing block
with pale green paint and test print once
or twice to remove excess paint. Using a
light hand, begin to print the leaves,
arranging them carefully in spray

formations as shown in the illustration.
Curve the spray of leaves into graceful
shapes and place them to suit the
contours of your project. Allow the paint
to dry thoroughly.

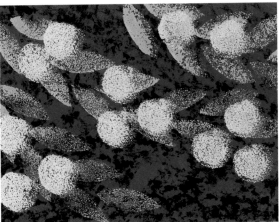

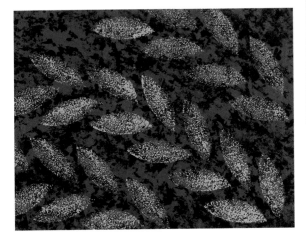

8 First print the peaches in a bright
yellow colour and then overprint with
peachy colours. The yellow paint will
show through the peachy colours,
giving additional texture and variety to
your work.

9 Print the peaches one by one, and for
variety, place some in groups of two or
three and others singly. If you wish,
overlap some of the fruits to form
clusters, just as you would find in
nature. Print as many peaches as you
like, but avoid overcrowding them.
While the paint is drying, wash and dry
the two printing blocks so that they are
ready for use.

10 Before beginning the next stage of
printing you will need to mix three

different shades of peach paint. Mix a
little bright yellow and scarlet paint into
white to create a very light shade of
peach. To create a medium shade of
peach, add a larger quantity of bright
yellow and scarlet paint to white.
Finally, mix a much brighter shade by
adding a small quantity of white paint
to bright yellow mixed with scarlet.

Coat the peach-shaped printing block
with the medium shade of peach. To
create the required contrast, add a dab
of the bright peach colour to one side of
the printing block and another of the
contrasting pale shade to the centre of
the block (see the colour guide for
reference). Test print once or twice to
blend the colours.

11 Print over the yellow circles, aligning
the printing block as carefully as
possible. Renew the contrasting colours
if they begin to fade. Continue until you
have overprinted all of the yellow
circles. Allow the paint to dry.

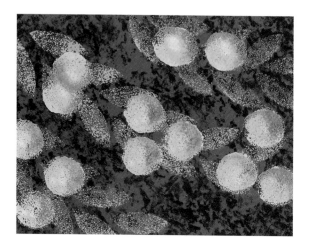

12 To paint the second layer of leaves you will need to mix several shades of green. Use bright yellow, dark blue, white and black to mix a variety of shades. Use a larger proportion of blue paint than yellow to ensure that all the colours are a bluish green and not too

yellow in tone. The range of colours you have mixed will then blend with the base colours and background.

Coat the leaf-shaped printing block with green paint. Test print once or twice but ensure that you do not remove too much paint as the density of printing needs to be quite heavy.

13 Begin to print the second layer of leaves, positioning them in the general direction of the first sprays that you printed. Be bold and experiment with your colours, adding light and dark shades to the sponge to give as much variety of colour as possible. Print a dense arrangement of leaves, all sweeping gracefully towards the left. Allow the paint to dry thoroughly.

Further Ideas and Options

This composition of fruits and foliage can be altered easily to represent different varieties of fruit. You can create apples and oranges without any changes to the printing blocks.

Oranges would need to have a slight shading of green paint on one side of the fruit and a lighter shade of orange to highlight the centre.

Apples could be printed using metallic paints. A deep russet red and a bright shade of green would blend into yellow to give the impression of a luscious, shiny fruit. Apples would look good nestled into a bright yellowish green foliage.

If you wish, you might adapt the printing blocks to reflect your own décor at home. With minor changes to the printing blocks, lemons, pears and other fruit could all be represented in a similar way. These projects would provide a good opportunity to experiment with colour and form.

CHAPTER 19

Forest Scene

Forest Scene

Decorated boxes and tins make attractive and individual gifts and, filled with little luxuries carefully chosen to suit the recipient, they become doubly appealing.

Toiletries, home-made chocolates, needlework sundries or packets of seeds could all be selected to fill your decorated boxes.

With simple alterations in colour, this design depicting a forest scene can be painted to represent the four seasons. A complete set of four boxes would make a very special present.

YOU WILL NEED
Basic equipment including three foam sponge pads

Additional Materials
Natural sea sponge
Sandpaper and wax polish

Paint
White
Dark blue (ultramarine)
Bright yellow (cadmium yellow)
Scarlet
Black
Yellow ochre

METHOD
1 Prepare and prime your project as described in Chapter 2

2 The distressed background effect is painted in green and cream. To paint the undercoat you will need to mix a dull green colour. Combine bright yellow and dark blue paint to create a medium shade of green. Add a little yellow ochre and a little black paint to create a sombre olive-green colour.

Paint your project with two coats of olive-green paint, allowing the paint to dry between coats.

3 Apply wax, following the guidelines for the distressed paint effect detailed in Chapter 7.

4 You will need to mix a cream colour to paint the topcoat. Begin by mixing a small amount of scarlet and green paint together to create a reddish brown colour. Add a small quantity of this brown paint to a larger quantity of white and then add a small amount of bright yellow. Blend these paints until you have achieved a rich creamy colour.

Paint your project with cream paint, applying two coats to cover the green base coat completely. Allow to dry.

5 Sandpaper your project to reveal a little of the green base coat.

6 To paint your forest scene, you will need to experiment freely with your paints to produce a variety of green shades. Use the following colours: dark blue, bright yellow, white, cream, black and yellow ochre to create a variety of subtle shades of green. In addition, you will be able to use the reddish brown colour that you mixed earlier to represent copper beech trees.

I have used fairly muted shades of green which give my little forest scene a slightly mysterious and brooding appearance, but if you prefer a lighter, sunnier effect, you may prefer to prepare much brighter colours when tackling your own work.

8 Study your project and decide where you wish the horizon to be positioned. Taking a piece of sea sponge, moisten it and then dip it into light green paint to sponge an impression of distant trees marking the horizon. Use a light hand when sponging and vary the colour as you work, sponging the impression of trees all the way round your project.

9 Mix a small amount of light mauve paint by adding scarlet and dark blue to white. Delicately sponge a little of this pale mauve colour amongst the green shades. Once you have finished this band of sponging, allow to dry.

10 Prepare the printing blocks as described in Chapter 5.

11 Coat the printing blocks with a variety of green shades. In order to represent the effect of sunlight on the trees, colour one side of each block with a lighter shade. As you work, ensure that your light and dark shades fall on the same sides of each block. This shading will lend a three-dimensional appearance to the flat shapes.

12 Now print the first layer of trees so that their tips just overlap the sponged horizon. Print the trees one by one, changing the colours on the printing blocks as you print each tree. When you have completed a row of trees framing your project, return to the beginning and overprint here and there with different shades, dark on light and light on dark. Use your piece of sea sponge to add texture to some of the trees and fill in any gaps. When you are happy with the results, allow the paint to dry.

provide stronger contrasts and increase the three-dimensional quality of your work. Once you have completed a second band of trees around your project, overprint and add texture as before. Allow the paint to dry.

13 Begin to print a second layer of trees, overlapping the first. To create a greater impression of distance, use stronger colours for this second layer of printing and apply more pressure to the sponges. Include some very dark-coloured trees in the second layer of printing to

14 Print a final layer of trees in an overlapping arrangement as before until the lower portion of your project is completely filled. Print more of the very dark-coloured cypress trees in the foreground of your picture to provide good, sharp contrasts of colour. Use your piece of sea sponge to add texture and, if necessary, fill in any remaining gaps. Allow the paint to dry thoroughly and clean your sponges.

15 Apply wax or varnish as required.

Further Ideas and Options

This forest scene can easily be adapted to represent the same trees viewed throughout the seasons.

Spring

Against a background of sky blue with sponged white clouds, use a palette of soft, fresh green shades for the trees, adding trees in pink and white blossom.

Summer

Against a background of cloudless bright blue sky, print the trees in bright shades of yellowish green.

Autumn

Sponge a palette of yellow, orange and red paint over a blue sky to represent a glowing sunset. Use beige, yellow, orange, red and brown to create a fiery mixture of autumn shades with which to print the trees.

Winter

Paint your background in a rich ultramarine blue. Add pinpoint dots of white paint to represent stars in the sky. Use frosty white paint on the printing blocks to create an impression of wintry, snow-laden trees.

CHAPTER 20

Goldfish Pond

Goldfish Pond

This colourful picture depicting an aerial view of a goldfish pond is surprisingly quick and easy to build up.

The image of shimmering blue water, golden fishes and delicate water lilies could be used to decorate any size of table top, toy-box or similar item of furniture.

The sponge paint effect in soft shades of green gives an impression of grassy foliage to the side of the project.

TOOLS AND MATERIALS
Basic equipment including two foam sponge pads

Additional Materials
Sheet foam measuring 12 x 12cm (4¾ x 4¾in)
Natural sea sponge
A small piece of bubble wrap

Paint
Dark blue (ultramarine)
Bright yellow (cadmium yellow)
White
Scarlet
Black
Blue pearl metallic acrylic paint
Periwinkle metallic acrylic paint
Pearl white metallic acrylic paint

METHOD
1 Prepare and prime your project as described in Chapter 2.

2 To undercoat the table legs or side of your project you will need to mix a light green paint. Combine dark blue and bright yellow paint and add a little white to lighten the colour.

Paint the lower part of your project light green, applying two or more coats to cover the priming paint. Allow the paint to dry thoroughly.

3 To undercoat the top of your project you will need to mix a pale blue colour. Mix a little dark blue paint into white to create a pale shade of blue. Paint the top of your project with pale blue paint, applying two or more coats to cover the priming paint. Put the project to one side to dry thoroughly.

4 You are now ready to create the watery effect on top of your project. Use a large watercolour brush to paint a watery mixture of blue pearl metallic paint over the pale blue base coat. Add some broad brushstrokes of a watery mixture of periwinkle metallic paint. Take a crumpled ball of kitchen paper

and sponge off some of the metallic paint, softening the dark blue lines and blending the colours together.

5 To create the grassy effect on the side of your project you will need to mix a variety of green shades. Use bright yellow, dark blue, white and black to create several light and dark shades of green. Using a piece of sea sponge and the sponging on method, sponge these green shades in a random pattern onto the side of your project.

6 Using the same method and the same green shades, sponge a band of foliage bordering the edge of your pond. Allow some strands of foliage to spill out over the water to give a natural appearance to the bank. Allow the paint to dry.

7 Prepare the printing blocks as described in Chapter 5. Cut the large water lily leaf shape from the piece of sheet foam and the smaller leaf from a sponge pad.

8 Coat the small daisy printing block with white paint and test print. Print the white daisies in small clusters on the green border surrounding your pond. Print as many groups of daisies as you wish. To complete these little flowers use a fine watercolour brush to add a dot to the centre of each flower in a colour of your choice.

9 To paint the pink flowers you will need to add a tiny amount of scarlet paint to white to create a pale pink shade. Coat the small circular printing block with the pale pink paint and add a spot of scarlet paint to the centre of the printing block (see the colour guide). Test print to blend the colours.

10 Print the little round flowers in dense clusters of blooms, on the green bank of your pond. Allow the paint to dry.

11 Use the sea sponge, dipped into green paint, to add a little more foliage overlapping some of the flowers. Allow the paint to dry.

12 Coat the water lily leaf printing blocks with light green paint. Add a contrast of darker green to the centre of each block (see the colour guide). Test print to blend the colours.

13 Use the two printing blocks to print a group of water lily leaves on the surface of your pond. Allow the paint to dry.

14 To paint the water lily flowers you will need to use the same shade of pale pink used for the small flowers. Coat the petal printing block with pale pink paint and add a contrast of scarlet to the tip of the petal (see the colour guide). Next, brush over the whole surface of the petal printing block with pearl white metallic paint. Test print to blend the colours. (The petals should have a very pale pink, pearly finish when the colours have blended together.)

15 Print seven slightly overlapping petals in a circular arrangement to form each bloom. The red tips, placed in the centre, will help to give an impression of depth to the flowers. Print as many flowers as you wish, renewing the colours frequently if they become indistinct. Allow the paint to dry and then use a fine watercolour brush to add a small yellow centre to each flower.

16 To paint the goldfish, begin by mixing bright yellow and scarlet paint to create a vivid shade of orange. Coat the fish-shaped printing block with orange paint and test print to blot any excess paint.

17 Print the fishes, grouping them into a graceful shoal. Allow the printing to become quite faint in places, so that it looks as if some of the fishes are well below the surface of the water. Print a few more of the fish motifs, singly or in small groups. Allow the paint to dry.

18 Use a fine watercolour brush to paint a watery mixture of periwinkle metallic paint around the outline of each water lily leaf and flower. Blend the paint outwards from the centre, and if necessary, using more water to dilute the colour until it becomes very pale and blends into the colour of the water.

You will find that by using this method the leaves and flowers stand out much more sharply than before. Allow the paint to dry thoroughly.

19 Apply a coat or two of varnish to protect your project from wear and tear – particularly if it is for a child!

Further Ideas and Options
A solid piece of furniture, such as a toy-box, could be painted to represent an aquarium with a host of exotic creatures, corals and plants inside. This provides ample opportunity to use a riot of colour for a young child to enjoy, or more subdued tones for an older child's room.

CHAPTER 21

Autumn Bouquet

Autumn Bouquet

Many of the printing blocks used in previous projects can be utilized in this composite design featuring autumn grasses, fruits and foliage.

With the introduction of several new motifs, the design is built up layer by layer, to create a colourful and unusual picture. The size of the design can be adapted to suit an individual project and the contents of the bouquet can be individually selected.

A single printed stem of physalis (Japanese lanterns) makes a striking small picture. It could equally be used to decorate a tall vase or similar project.

TOOLS AND MATERIALS
Basic equipment including three foam sponge pads

Additional Materials
Strong card, hardboard, or a ready prepared oil-painting board (Hardboard will need to be primed with several coats of emulsion paint to prevent the paint from sinking into the porous surface.)
Natural sea sponge

Paint
Dark blue (ultramarine)
Bright yellow (cadmium yellow)
Scarlet
Black
White
Yellow ochre
Cream
Pearl white metallic acrylic paint
Bronze metallic acrylic paint

METHOD
1 Prepare and prime your project if necessary.

2 You will need to mix a dark brown colour to paint the background to the design. Combine bright yellow and dark blue paint to create a medium shade of green and then add a roughly equal quantity of scarlet paint. Adjust the colours if necessary and then add a little black paint to darken the colour.

3 Paint your project with the dark brown paint, applying two or more coats to ensure good, even coverage. While the last coat of paint is still wet, use the sea sponge to apply a little medium green paint to the lower third of the project. The green paint will blend into the brown to create a subtle colour variation at the base of your project. Allow the paint to dry.

4 Prepare the printing blocks as described in Chapter 5.

5 Study your project and decide what size and shape you would like your bouquet to be. The sponged grasses form a framework for the design and can be expanded or contracted to fit any size or shape of project. All the printed motifs can then be placed within this grassy framework.

6 Use the sea sponge to paint in the fan-shaped arrangement of grasses. Use yellow ochre, cream and white paint to sponge on an impression of a bird's feathery plumes. Keep the sponging as light and delicate as possible. While the paint is still wet, sponge a little darker brown paint over some of this.

7 Mix a little cream paint into the dark brown and use this to sponge a fan-shaped arrangement of brown, feathery plumes in the lower half of your project. Although ultimately you will see little of this sponging, the impression of dark foliage will be glimpsed between the printed motifs and will help to make the bouquet appear 'solid'. When you have completed this sponging, allow the paint to dry.

8 Coat the poppy head printing block with yellow ochre paint. Add a contrast of cream paint to one side of the block (see the colour guide).

9 Print as many poppy seed heads as you wish, positioning them to fill the spaces between the grassy plumes. Allow the printing to become quite faint in some places to give a variety of textures to the seed heads. Allow to dry.

10 Coat the oval-shaped honesty printing block with pearl white metallic paint and test print several times to blot excess paint.

11 Space the honesty seed heads irregularly, within the framework of your design.

12 Use a fine, watercolour brush to paint a tiny pearl-white point at the top of each oval-shaped seed head. Allow the paint to dry.

13 The physalis (Japanese lanterns) will form the focal point of your design. Take as much time as you need to decide how many of these motifs you will print and how best to position them. You'll achieve maximum impact if you arrange the Japanese lanterns to form a balanced shape within the centre of your bouquet.

14 The Japanese lanterns are printed in two separate stages. The large berry is printed first and allowed to dry, before the 'lantern' is overprinted. The lanterns need to be fairly faint and delicate to allow the berry to show through clearly. This will create a very accurate impression of the way in which these physalis seedpods skeletonize as they wither and dry.

15 You will need to mix bright yellow and scarlet paint together to create a bright shade of orange.Coat the berry-shaped printing block with orange paint and add a dot of white paint to represent a shiny highlight (see the colour guide).

16 Print a berry in each of the positions you have allocated for the lanterns. Renew the white dot frequently if it becomes indistinct. When you have printed all the berries, set the project aside to dry.

17 Coat the Japanese lantern-shaped printing blocks with orange paint and test print until the printing becomes very faint. The smaller lanterns are best placed towards the top of the picture, the larger ones nearer the base.

18 Print a lantern over each berry, positioning them so that they are tilted in different directions. Allow the paint to dry thoroughly.

19 Now you can experiment freely with leaves and berries to fill any spaces in the centre of your bouquet. Select any of the leaf shapes used in previous projects and print them in autumnal shades of red, gold and brown. Include some

holly, mistletoe berries and other berries if you wish. Add a white highlight to these as described for holly.

20 When you have completed the central portion of your design and are happy with the results, use the sea sponge to add a few more feathery grasses to any gaps in the design. Add a few light touches of the sponge in the background of the design to 'soften' the framework. Finally, dip the sponge into bronze metallic paint and apply a few light touches of bronze to add a little 'sparkle' to the design. Put the project aside and allow the paint to dry thoroughly.

21 Apply one or two coats of wax or varnish to your project.

Further Ideas and Options

A large project, such as a fire screen, provides an opportunity to add different motifs to the basic design. You might like to use bulrushes, rosehips, thistles, or dried flower heads. Butterflies or other insects could also be included.

CHAPTER 22

Templates and Colour Guides

Moon and Stars

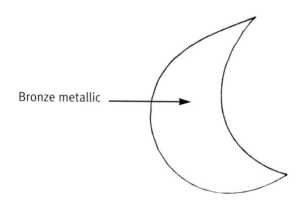

Bronze metallic

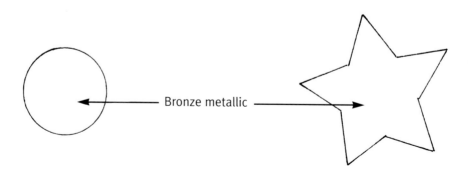

Bronze metallic

Flowerpot Designs

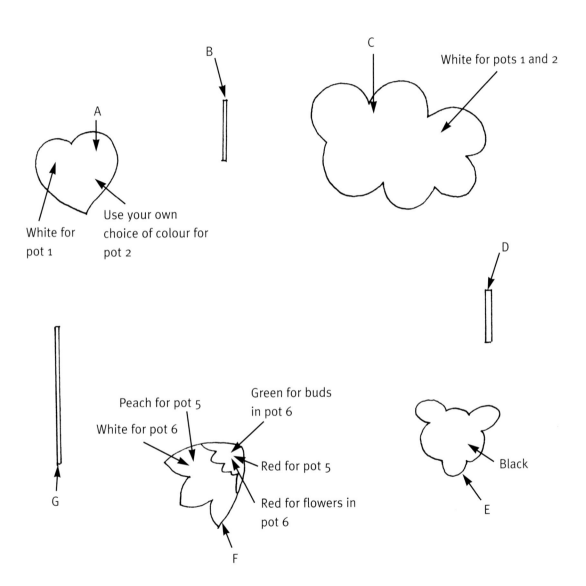

B

C

White for pots 1 and 2

A

Use your own
choice of colour for
pot 2

White for
pot 1

D

Green for buds
in pot 6

Peach for pot 5

White for pot 6

Red for pot 5

Red for flowers in
pot 6

Black

G

F

E

The strips B, D and G are 1cm (½in) deep. It is not necessary to provide a stiff base material on small printing blocks like these.

Leaves and Cherries

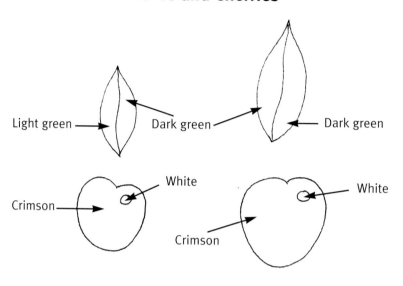

Light green ——>   <—— Dark green   Dark green

White

Crimson ———>

White

Crimson

Christmas Design

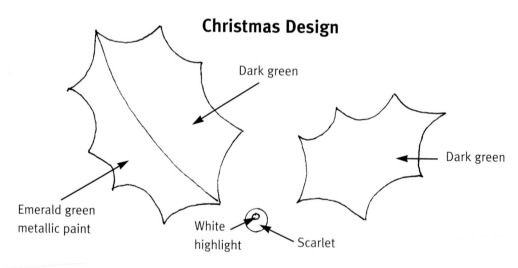

Dark green

Dark green

Emerald green
metallic paint

White
highlight   Scarlet

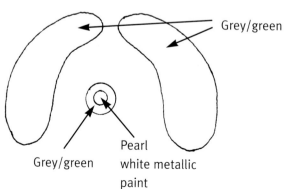

Grey/green

Grey/green   Pearl
white metallic
paint

Climbing Ivy

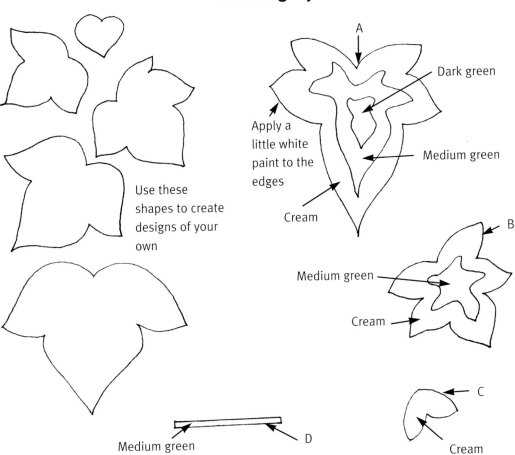

Use these shapes to create designs of your own

Apply a little white paint to the edges

A

Dark green

Medium green

Cream

B

Medium green

Cream

C

Cream

Medium green D

Flowers and Bees

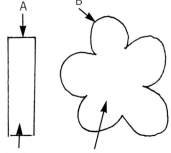
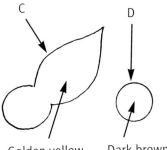

A

B

C

D

E

F

Dark green
Light green

Bright orange

Golden yellow

Dark brown

Dark brown

Pearl white metallic paint

Sunflowers

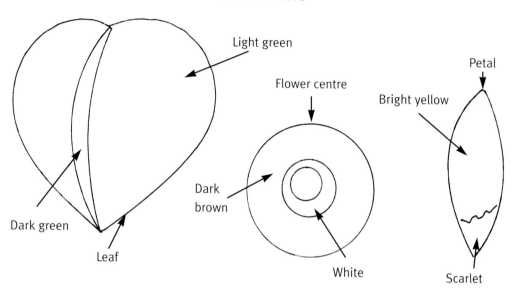

Vine Design

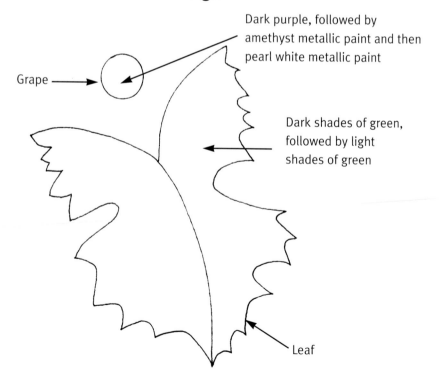

Bamboo and Butterflies

Light shades of grey/green
and blue/green

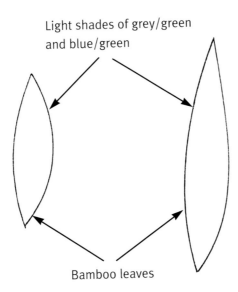

Bamboo leaves

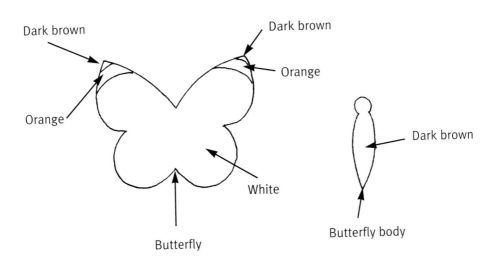

Dark brown

Dark brown

Orange

Orange

Dark brown

White

Butterfly

Butterfly body

Clematis Design

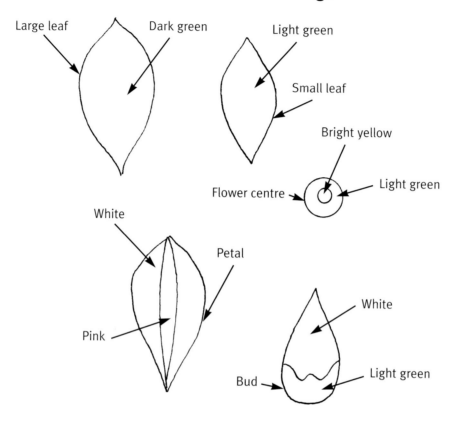

Peaches

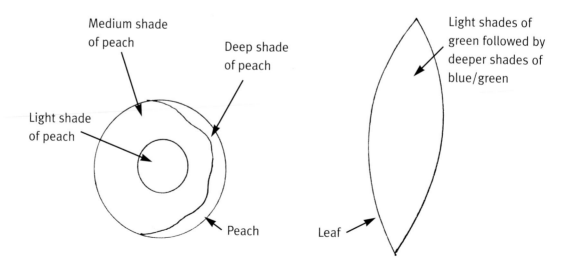

Forest Scene

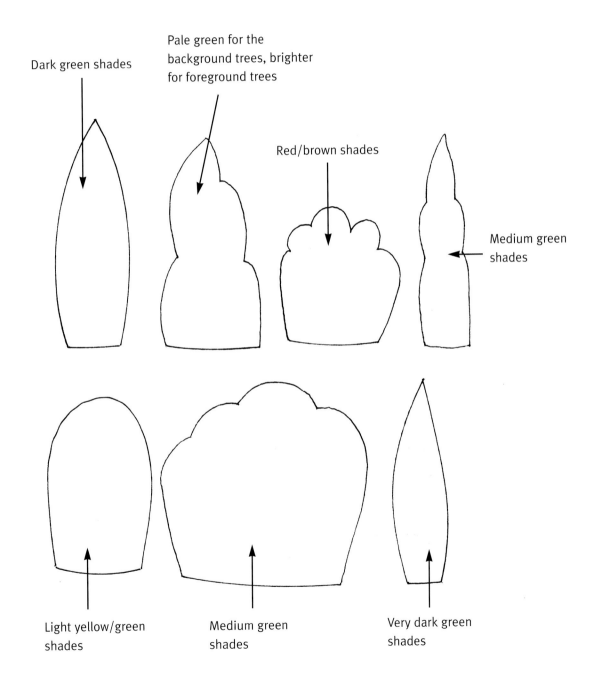

Dark green shades

Pale green for the background trees, brighter for foreground trees

Red/brown shades

Medium green shades

Light yellow/green shades

Medium green shades

Very dark green shades

Photocopy at 127% for original size

Goldfish Pond

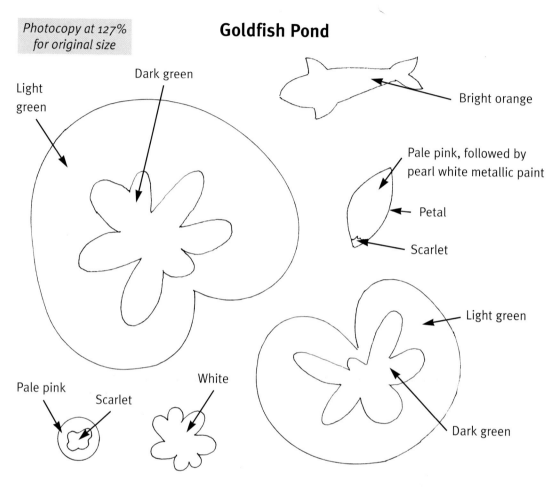

Light green

Dark green

Bright orange

Pale pink, followed by pearl white metallic paint

Petal

Scarlet

Light green

Dark green

Pale pink

Scarlet

White

Autumn Bouquet

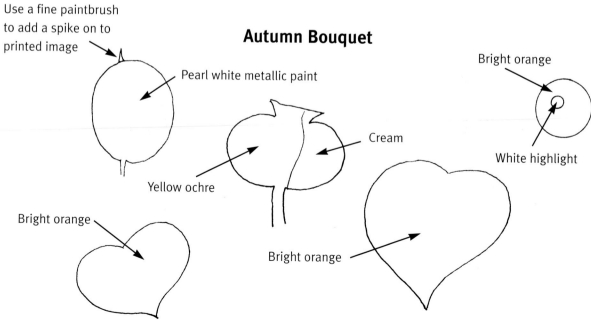

Use a fine paintbrush to add a spike on to printed image

Pearl white metallic paint

Bright orange

White highlight

Cream

Yellow ochre

Bright orange

Bright orange

About the Author

Ann Rooney completed a foundation course in art and design, and another in textiles which introduced her to a variety of printing techniques from lino-cutting to lithography, Batik and silk-screen printing. She has spent many years teaching arts and crafts to people with physical disabilities. In recent years, Ann has sold her sponge painting at craft fairs and this book is a response to all those fascinated customers who have asked 'How is it done?'. She has had a lifelong interest in and love of the natural world and her garden is her biggest source of inspiration.

Index

TITLES AVAILABLE FROM
GMC PUBLICATIONS
BOOKS

WOODWORKING

40 More Woodworking Plans & Projects	*GMC Publications*
Bird Boxes and Feeders for the Garden	*Dave Mackenzie*
Complete Woodfinishing	*Ian Hosker*
David Charlesworth's Furniture-making Techniques	*David Charlesworth*
Electric Woodwork	*Jeremy Broun*
Furniture & Cabinetmaking Projects	*GMC Publications*
Furniture Projects	*Rod Wales*
Furniture Restoration (Practical Crafts)	*Kevin Jan Bonner*
Furniture Restoration and Repair for Beginners	*Kevin Jan Bonner*
Furniture Restoration Workshop	*Kevin Jan Bonner*
Green Woodwork	*Mike Abbott*
Making & Modifying Woodworking Tools	*Jim Kingshott*
Making Chairs and Tables	*GMC Publications*
Making Fine Furniture	*Tom Darby*
Making Little Boxes from Wood	*John Bennett*
Making Shaker Furniture	*Barry Jackson*
Making Woodwork Aids and Devices	*Robert Wearing*
Minidrill: 15 Projects	*John Everett*
Pine Furniture Projects for the Home	*Dave Mackenzie*
Routing for Beginners	*Anthony Bailey*
Router Magic: Jigs, Fixtures and Tricks to Unleash your Router's Full Potential	*Bill Hylton*
Router Projects for the Home	*GMC Publications*
The Scrollsaw: Twenty Projects	*John Everett*
Sharpening Pocket Reference Book	*Jim Kingshott*
Sharpening: The Complete Guide	*Jim Kingshott*
Space-Saving Furniture Projects	*Dave Mackenzie*
Stickmaking: A Complete Course	*Andrew Jones & Clive George*
Stickmaking Handbook	*Andrew Jones & Clive George*
Test Reports: *The Router* and *Furniture & Cabinetmaking*	*GMC Publications*
Veneering: A Complete Course	*Ian Hosker*
Woodfinishing Handbook (Practical Crafts)	*Ian Hosker*
Woodworking Plans and Projects	*GMC Publications*
Woodworking with the Router: Professional Router Techniques any Woodworker can Use	*Bill Hylton & Fred Matlack*
The Workshop	*Jim Kingshott*

WOODTURNING

Adventures in Woodturning	*David Springett*
Bert Marsh: Woodturner	*Bert Marsh*
Bill Jones' Notes from the Turning Shop	*Bill Jones*
Bill Jones' Further Notes from the Turning Shop	*Bill Jones*
Bowl Turning Masterclass	*Tony Boase*
Colouring Techniques for Woodturners	*Jan Sanders*
The Craftsman Woodturner	*Peter Child*
Decorative Techniques for Woodturners	*Hilary Bowen*
Essential Tips for Woodturners	*GMC Publications*
Faceplate Turning	*GMC Publications*
Fun at the Lathe	*R.C. Bell*
Further Useful Tips for Woodturners	*GMC Publications*
Illustrated Woodturning Techniques	*John Hunnex*
Intermediate Woodturning Projects	*GMC Publications*
Keith Rowley's Woodturning Projects	*Keith Rowley*
Make Money from Woodturning	*Ann & Bob Phillips*
Multi-Centre Woodturning	*Ray Hopper*
Pleasure and Profit from Woodturning	*Reg Sherwin*
Practical Tips for Turners & Carvers	*GMC Publications*
Practical Tips for Woodturners	*GMC Publications*
Spindle Turning	*GMC Publications*
Turning Miniatures in Wood	*John Sainsbury*
Turning Wooden Toys	*Terry Lawrence*
Turning Pens & Pencils	*Kip Christensen & Rex Burningham*
Understanding Woodturning	*Ann & Bob Phillips*
Useful Techniques for Woodturners	*GMC Publications*
Useful Woodturning Projects	*GMC Publications*
Woodturning: Bowls, Platters, Hollow Forms, Vases, Vessels, Bottles, Flasks, Tankards, Plates	*GMC Publications*
Woodturning: A Foundation Course (New Edition)	*Keith Rowley*
Woodturning: A Fresh Approach	*Robert Chapman*
Woodturning: A Source Book of Shapes	*John Hunnex*
Woodturning Jewellery	*Hilary Bowen*
Woodturning Masterclass	*Tony Boase*
Woodturning Techniques	*GMC Publications*
Woodturning Tools & Equipment Test Reports	*GMC Publications*
Woodturning Wizardry	*David Springett*

WOODCARVING

The Art of the Woodcarver	*GMC Publications*
Carving Birds & Beasts	*GMC Publications*
Carving on Turning	*Chris Pye*
Carving Realistic Birds	*David Tippey*
Decorative Woodcarving	*Jeremy Williams*
Essential Tips for Woodcarvers	*GMC Publications*
Essential Woodcarving Techniques	*Dick Onians*
Lettercarving in Wood: A Practical Course	*Chris Pye*
Power Tools for Woodcarving	*David Tippey*
Practical Tips for Turners & Carvers	*GMC Publications*
Relief Carving in Wood: A Practical Introduction	*Chris Pye*
Understanding Woodcarving	*GMC Publications*
Understanding Woodcarving in the Round	*GMC Publications*
Useful Techniques for Woodcarvers	*GMC Publications*
Wildfowl Carving - Volume 1	*Jim Pearce*
Wildfowl Carving - Volume 2	*Jim Pearce*
The Woodcarvers	*GMC Publications*
Woodcarving: A Complete Course	*Ron Butterfield*
Woodcarving: A Foundation Course	*Zoë Gertner*
Woodcarving for Beginners	*GMC Publications*
Woodcarving Tools & Equipment Test Reports	*GMC Publications*
Woodcarving Tools, Materials & Equipment	*Chris Pye*

UPHOLSTERY

Seat Weaving (Practical Crafts)	*Ricky Holdstock*
Upholsterer's Pocket Reference Book	*David James*
Upholstery: A Complete Course (Revised Edition)	*David James*
Upholstery Restoration	*David James*
Upholstery Techniques & Projects	*David James*

MAGAZINES

**Woodturning • Woodcarving • Furniture & Cabinetmaking • The Dolls' House Magazine
The Router • The ScrollSaw • Creative Crafts for the Home • BusinessMatters • Water Gardening**

The above represents a full list of all titles currently published or scheduled to be published.
All are available direct from the Publishers or through bookshops, newsagents and specialist retailers.
To place an order, or to obtain a complete catalogue, contact:

GMC Publications

Castle Place, 166 High Street, Lewes, East Sussex BN7 1XU, United Kingdom Tel: 01273 488005 Fax: 01273 478606
Orders by credit card are accepted

DISCARDED
Easthampton, MA 01027